THE
GALVESTON DISPATCHES

THE
GALVESTON DISPATCHES

A Swiss Missionary's Account
of Nineteenth-Century Texas

Fred Huddleston and Clay Rogers

Published by The History Press
Charleston, SC
www.historypress.com

Copyright © 2025 by Fred Huddleston and Clay Rogers

Opposite: Fred Huddleston, translator/author. *Courtesy of author.*

First published 2025

Manufactured in the United States

ISBN 9781467158718

Library of Congress Control Number: 2024947497

This book is dedicated to the memory of Fred Harley Huddleston,
who started the journey of translating Friedrich Gloor's letters.
I was honored to complete the project.

CONTENTS

CONTENTS

PREFACE

I t has been said that every person's life is worth a novel. Most never get written. This is but a piece of Friedrich Gloor's novel.

At the age of nineteen, Friedrich left his home in Basel, Switzerland, where he taught school at an orphanage. He had been sent by the Basel Pilgermission St. Chrischona Institute halfway around the world to teach at the First (German) Evangelical Lutheran Church in Galveston, Texas. After a seventy-five-day sea voyage, he arrived in Galveston on April 8, 1855.

Friedrich sent letters to his family in Basel describing in beautiful detail his adventures, triumphs and trials across Texas and Louisiana from his arrival until 1866. Most of Friedrich's letters concern his experiences in Galveston. The letters were discovered in 2006 by Alain Moriandat, the Swiss president of the International League of Antiquarian Booksellers. Moriandat donated the letters to the University Library of Basel (Abteilung G IV 117) in 2011. The university determined that since the letters primarily describe Galveston's history, they should be sent to the Rosenberg Library in Galveston. From there the letters were given to Galveston's First Evangelical Lutheran Church, which then provided them to Fred Huddleston to translate and explore Friedrich's adventures. Like Friedrich, these letters have traveled far.

The St. Chrischona Institute in Basel still exists at the highest point in northwest Switzerland on a site regarded as holy since the fifth century. In the 1800s, the St. Chrischona Institute sent 121 missionaries of the early Lutheran Church, pastors and teachers, including Friedrich, to Texas.

Original letter written in Swiss German by Friedrich Gloor. *Courtesy of University Library of Basel, G IV 117 archives.*

Friedrich was an eloquent and gifted writer. The content of letters to his "parents and siblings" stretches over a period of eleven years. In his letters, he gives a detailed account of his life and experiences in Galveston, as well as the local landscape, the way of life on the island and important events. In addition to his personal experiences, he reports on life in the Christian

Photograph of the tall ship *Elissa*, a three-masted barque launched in 1877. This is likely quite similar to the ship on which Gloor would have sailed to Galveston. *Courtesy of the Galveston Historical Foundation.*

community, his marriage to Therese Wunscher (1859), his financial circumstances and debts owed to his homeland, shipwrecks and the fate of early settler families. He also describes historical events such as slavery and the Civil War, the Battle of Galveston and the subsequent rough period of Reconstruction. However, Friedrich was haunted by his past—an event or experience that took place in his early days in Basel. He speaks of it frequently. We may never know what tormented him and caused him to continually ask for forgiveness, and the reader of these letters is left to their own imagination.

Importantly, Friedrich describes how the First Lutheran Church was established in Galveston and other parts of Texas and the important role the St. Chrischona missionaries played in establishing the congregations.

Right: Photograph of Reverend Friedrich Gloor.

Middle: St. Chrischona Chapel and surrounding buildings. *From* A Centennial Story of the Lutheran Church, 1851–1951.

Bottom: An 1855 bird's-eye view of Galveston, the year before Gloor arrived. *Courtesy of the Rosenberg Library.*

In 1864, during the American Civil War, Friedrich was named pastorate of First Evangelical Lutheran Church and was formally ordained pastor in 1867. Under his leadership, a new Lutheran church was built in 1868 and still stands today. Friedrich died in Galveston in 1876, while still serving as pastor. He was the last of the Chrischona missionaries to serve the church. He died ten years after he wrote the last known letter to his family.

ACKNOWLEDGEMENTS

I would like to acknowledge the generosity of the University Library of Basel (G IV 117) for preserving this history in the 16 Briefe an Eltern und Geschwister (swisscollections.ch) (Gloor letters) and providing them first to the Rosenberg Library of Galveston to allow us to understand Friedrich's life and experience in Galveston and the Lutheran Church in the 1850s and 1860s.

Also, I would like to acknowledge the Rosenberg Library of Galveston for its courtesy and assistance in providing relevant images, photographs and maps for this book, as well as providing the German written letters to Fred Huddleston. The Rosenberg Library is one of the finest archives and repositories of manuscript materials in the Southwest and fully deserves its excellent reputation.

The Galveston Historical Foundation (GHF) deserves much credit for encouraging me to publish these letters and providing guidance and direction regarding the history of Galveston, as well as furnishing images from its archives. A special thanks goes to GHF's Dwayne Jones, executive director/chief executive officer, and Jami Durham, historian (property research and cultural history), for their invaluable assistance. The Galveston Historical Foundation has worked tirelessly for more than fifty years to preserve the rich history of the city and saved many of its historical structures that otherwise would have been lost to decay and neglect.

And thank you to Pastor Richard Rhodes of First Evangelical Church of Galveston for your thoughtful input, wisdom and source material.

THE ESTABLISHMENT
OF LUTHERANISM AND THE
ST. CHRISCHONA INSTITUTE

T o understand Friedrich Gloor, one must understand his background in Lutheranism and the Basel, Switzerland St. Chrischona Institute, where he studied and taught. These building blocks made Friedrich who he was.

MARTIN LUTHER AND
THE BEGINNINGS OF LUTHERANISM

Lutheranism traces its roots back to the Protestant Reformation of the sixteenth century, which was initiated by Martin Luther, a German monk and theologian.

Martin Luther, troubled by what he saw as corruption and doctrinal deviations within the Roman Catholic Church, famously posted his "95 theses" on the door of the Castle Church in Wittenberg, Germany, on October 31, 1517. This act is often regarded as the starting point of the Reformation. Luther's writings and teachings challenged various practices and beliefs of the Catholic Church, including the sale of indulgences and the doctrine of salvation by works. His ideas spread rapidly throughout Europe, leading to the formation of new religious movements.

Luther's teachings gained popularity, particularly in German-speaking territories and the Scandinavian countries. Princes and rulers who supported Luther's ideas established Lutheranism as the official religion in their

Left: Painting of Martin Luther, founder of Lutheranism in the sixteenth century.

Below: Image of Martin Luther posting his "95 theses" on doors in Germany in 1517.

domains. Due to the creation of the Guttenberg press, the translation of the Bible into vernacular languages, particularly German, played a significant role in spreading Luther's ideas to the common people.

Martin Luther remains one of the most influential figures in the history of Christianity.

ST. CHRISCHONA INSTITUTE'S MISSION AND BEGINNING

The church of St. Chrischona is located in the municipality of Bettingen, Switzerland. It is here where Gloor began his studies and teaching. The church sits half a mile above sea level at the highest point of the canton of Basel-Stadt. The site has been considered holy since the fifth century. Presumably the first church was built in the seventh century and expanded and enlarged in the eighth and ninth centuries. During the Thirty Years' War (1618–48), the church was desecrated and plundered by Swedish troops. The church was increasingly neglected and even used as a stable in 1818.

In the nineteenth century, a new Romanesque building was constructed in place of the Carolingian church, probably still without a tower but with a churchyard where the dead of Bettingen were buried. Probably the church

St. Chrischona Chapel after its restoration. *From* A Centennial Story of the Lutheran Church, 1851–1951.

was originally more dedicated to St. Brictius of Tours, as indicated by old names in the area. If remembered at all, St. Brictius has become virtually synonymous with the recorded mass execution of Danes that took place under the orders of King Æthelred "the Unready" on his feast day in 1002, an event now known simply the "St. Brice's Day Massacre."[1]

In the nineteenth century, the legend of St. Chrischona was created, which also led to popular pilgrimages taking place to St. Chrischona.

In 1839, Christian Friedrich Spittler (April 12, 1782–December 8, 1867) received permission to renovate the church. In 1840, the pilgrimage mission of St. Chrischona was founded by Spittler and still exists today.

Painting of Christian Friedrich Spittler, founder of the St. Chrischona Pilgrimage Mission, credited for establishing the German Lutheran church in Texas.

The St. Chrischona Pilgrimage Mission was built on the tenets of Lutheranism and Calvinism. Under Spittler's leadership, the mission society began work among German emigrants in Texas. It was these early St. Chrischona missionaries who established the Lutheran Church in Texas and specifically Galveston.

After sixty-six years of work in Basel, Spittler died at the age of eighty-five.

THE INTRODUCTION OF LUTHERANISM INTO THE UNITED STATES

Records indicate that Lutherans had early contacts in the New World as Jamestown, Virginia (1607), and Plymouth, Massachusetts (1620), were being colonized. In contrast to the French and Spaniards, the English-speaking colonists were mostly Protestants, including Lutherans.[2]

In the early decades of the nineteenth century, political unrest gripped Europe. The Germans longed for civil liberty, freedom and a united German state, and this led to rebellion. Many German men who joined the freedom fighters were forced to flee the fatherland, and so in the latter half of the 1840s, the number of German immigrants increased rapidly. The spouses usually came later to join their husbands in establishing new homes here. The industry of the county began to expand, and as opportunities for employment increased, so did the stream of newcomers.

In September 1852, Reverend Theobald Kleis came to Johnstown, and a new era in the religious life of the Germans began. Pastor Kleis had been a catechist in the St. Chrischona Institute near Basel. After an urgent request was made for missionaries to Texas, he landed in Galveston in 1850 and organized churches in Sequin, San Antonio, Castorville and Braunfels.

In 1852, Pastor Kleis obtained permission to go north to solicit financial support for the work in Texas among the congregations of the Pittsburgh, Pennsylvania Synod. It is most likely that because of his success in Texas, he was persuaded by Dr. William A. Passavant, the great missionary pioneer of the Pittsburgh Synod, to stay and look after the scattered German Lutherans in the Johnstown area.

First (German) Evangelical Lutheran Church in Galveston Is Established

The beginnings of First (German) Evangelical Lutheran Church of Galveston, Texas, were laid in the Lutheran Missionary Seminary of St. Chrischona. The flag of Texas had scarcely been unfurled when missionaries came and planted the banner of the cross beside it. When Texas became a republic, favorable terms were offered to all those who would settle the new republic. Many of these colonists who came were Lutherans and helped to establish the oldest Lutheran churches in Texas. However, there was a void in spiritual leadership at the time. In 1849, a certain Christian gentleman wrote to his relatives in Switzerland complaining of this void. The plea from Texas was communicated to Dr. Christian Splitter, dean of the Lutheran Missionary Seminary near Basel. Thus it came about that two young Lutheran pastors, Reverend Theobald Kleis and Reverend Adam Sager, were dispatched to Texas. The original church in Galveston was a gathering of seven Lutheran families into a congregation. So 1850 was the beginning of this Lutheran church, known then as the First German Evangelical Church of Galveston, Texas, and chartered by the State of Texas in 1851.[3]

Soon after the organization of this congregation in 1850, Reverend Guebner departed for other mission fields in 1851, but more Chrischona men arrived in Texas. St. Chrischona sent the six pastors, their entire 1851

An 1839 city view of Galveston. *Courtesy of the Texas State Library.*

graduating class, to Texas: John George Ebinger, Christian Oefinger, John Conrad Roehm, William T. Strobel, Henry Wendt and Philipp Frederick Zizelmann. Each one was destined to become pastor of First Evangelical Lutheran Church in Galveston.[4]

They immediately discovered that Pastor Guebner had departed, leaving no instructions. Not a soul was expecting the six missionaries. The seven congregation families provided the missionaries lodging. Pastor Wendt stayed in Galveston to serve that congregation. The other five traveled by boat to Houston to consult with Pastor Caspar Braun.

So Reverend H. Wendt was the first of these six to take charge of the congregation in 1851. The first thing Wendt did was start a school, to be maintained by the church. Friedrich Gloor arrived in 1855 and was assigned

to teach at the church school. The Wendt family brought him into their home, and Gloor wrote of the development of their close friendship.

In 1854, arrangements were made for holding Sunday services in the Lyceum Hall, located on the corner of Winnie and Bath Avenue (25th Street). This hall belonged to the Lyceum Association, founded in 1840, and was the center of culture in Galveston. Prior to holding services in the Lyceum Hall, as church records indicate, services were most likely held in the Lutheran school. The church prospered under Pastor Wendt; membership increased, and financial hardships were met and overcome.

As Gloor described in his letters, First Lutheran bought the Lyceum Hall and moved it to the present church property. Today, the old Lyceum building is preserved in the west wing of the church and functions as a beautifully restored events space, with seven pairs of original stained-glass windows installed in 1915.

An 1871 bird's-eye view of Galveston. *Courtesy of the Rosenberg Library.*

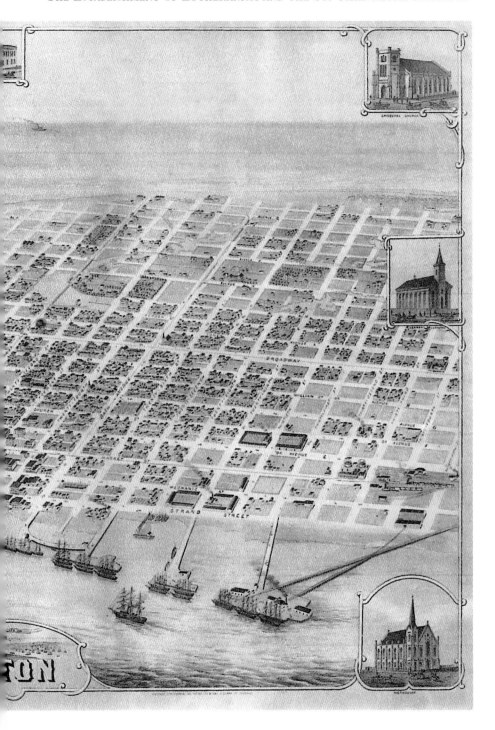

Left: Detail of the 1871 bird's-eye view of Galveston, showing the First Evangelical Lutheran Church. *Courtesy of the Rosenberg Library.*

Below: Photograph of the First Evangelical Lutheran Church, 1868. *Courtesy of First Evangelical Lutheran Church Galveston, Texas.*

In 1856, Reverend Wendt returned to Europe to visit his homeland just prior to the bombardment of Galveston during the Civil War. There is no evidence that Wendt ever returned. The church was without a pastor from 1856 until 1959, when it called J.G. Ebinger as its ordained pastor. In 1864, in the midst of the Civil War, the church was left without a pastor, and it was difficult to find a replacement. Gloor was urged to take over the ministry and reluctantly agreed. But as Gloor explained, he believed in his heart that he was called to teach, not preach. After Gloor consented, he was ordained in Brenham, Texas, in November 1866 and served the church until his death on November 11, 1876.

Many changes occurred during the pastorate of Reverend Gloor. The city and state recovered rapidly from the ravages of the Civil War, and so did the congregation. The island population grew. The Lyceum Building became too small to hold the growing congregation.[5] It was during Reverend Gloor's pastorate that the congregation passed a resolution to erect a new church. The church was competed in 1868, with a larger, more imposing edifice. Work on the new building was rushed, and services were held in the new church in May 1868.[6] So it was that Gloor is credited for building the First Evangelical Lutheran Church in Galveston.

Friedrich Gloor, first as a teacher and later a pastor, wrote in beautiful detail of his experiences in Galveston, New Orleans and Central Texas and the beginnings of the Lutheran Church on the island. While we do not know what happened to Gloor's communications with his family after 1866, it is likely that they were never discovered. However, his letters between 1855 and 1866 are a treasure-trove of details of day-to-day life, hardships and triumphs.

GLOOR'S LETTERS[7]

THE TEXAS CLIMATE

Yellow Fever and a Hanging [8]

In the 1850s, the German Lutheran Congregation Church was considered one of the most prosperous and useful institutions of learning in Galveston. The original church building itself was moved after Friedrich arrived. It was built as the Lyceum Building in 1846 and moved from a neighboring site and leased by the church for special functions. It is here where the first church services were likely held. Friedrich related his initial impression of Galveston—how low and flat the ground was and how water covers everything whenever there is a storm.

In June 1955, shortly after his arrival, Friedrich witnessed the frontier's "justice" in the hanging of a man and the mistreatment of enslaved people, including death by fire. Yellow fever was rampant in New Orleans and Galveston, and Friedrich contracted the disease his first year on the island but survived to continue his historical journals to his family.

Here Friedrich begins his first letter to his Swiss home.

❧

Mr. C. Gloor, No 754 L, Kanonengasse in Basel.

Galveston the 9th of May, 1855.

I am asking Mr. Spittler [*Christian Friedrich Spittler, 1782–1867, head of St. Chrischona Institute in Basel*], to whom I am extending warm greetings to he and his entire family, to send this letter to my father at the above address. Friedrich Gloor

My dear parents and siblings!

For the second time I send you my deepest and most heartfelt greetings from far away, across the ocean, and I pray to God that my greetings find you all well and happy. In my last letter,[9] it was impossible for me to send you anything definite about my new home, where I live without more travels, with my dear friend and brother, Pastor Wendt. Since my last letter, my future has been changed quite a bit because brother Lieb, who lead the German school here, was sent through various circumstances, deeper into the countryside.

On April 23, I began as a teacher at the German school here. I have about 30 children at the school, and I teach uninterrupted from 8 a.m. until 2 p.m. We came to this arrangement because between 11 a.m. and 2 p.m. are the hottest times of the day and going out into the sun at that time carries significant dangers. From 2 p.m. on I can preoccupy myself with various things, partly getting the next day ready, including getting the English hour lesson ready for some young people I teach. Maybe I can soon start giving French lessons as well. I live with Pastor Wendt, who owns the school, and with whom I am very closely connected. We feel like brothers to one another. I have a room, food and laundry etc. and am considered as a member of the family. Pastor Wendt's family consists of his wife, a dear little girl and an adopted child. Saturday I have entirely to myself. On Sunday I am a verger, and on Sunday afternoon we either make visits or have walks to the beach, which are the only walks one can do on our small island. My health is now so satisfactory, that I cannot thank the dear Lord enough for my happiness, especially since the climate here is generally very unhealthy. During the first fourteen days of my arrival I had various ills, with fever, body aches, toothaches, etc. These were great trials, but it was all part of the normal process of acclamation and now these problems have totally disappeared. That's the news so far about my external circumstances. I have, once again, a sphere of influence, and have returned to a normal, orderly lifestyle. I know again why I am in this world. I feel content and even though the thoughts of my past arise frequently, the view to the future and the certain hope is that with the help of God I will be able to catch up and make right many things of my past. The dear Lord will certainly make right by me, otherwise he would not have led me through storm, illness, hunger and the many difficulties and hardships to make me so happy in this beautiful land.

It will be interesting for you to learn a few things about the land where I live now. The whole of Texas is about 20 times the size of Switzerland, but only one ninth of the population of Switzerland. The city of Galveston lies not far from the coast of Texas on an island. The island is 12 hours long but only ¾ of an hour wide, and consists entirely of fine sand. All around us day and night we hear the sound of the waves of the Gulf of Mexico. The island is so flat and shallow that during the times of storm the whole island is flooded. Galveston is no larger in size than Basel but it has only 8000 inhabitants. There are many Germans, French, Spanish, and Negros (most which are slaves). The houses here are very small, and always have a courtyard and a garden, which is surrounded by a picket fence, which they call "fenz" here. Since not a single stone can be found on the whole island except for the ones brought in by ships, the houses are built entirely out of wood but don't stand on the ground but on a number of wooden blocks, which are placed on the ground. Therefore, there is a hollow space between the house and the ground, which allows the water to run off during heavy rains. If this was not done, the houses would deteriorate from below within a few years. If one doesn't like the place where one's house is located, one simply buys another piece of land and then wheels are attached on the house or the house is placed on rolls and pulled through the streets to its new location. They call that here "a house movin". Just before my arrival the community had bought a beautiful, large house, to use it as a church. They bought the house for its beauty and size and they also bought a different piece of land, right next to the school. Then the church was moved on wheels to this new location next to the school and at the same time turned around to face a different direction.

The apartment of Brother Wendt consists of small houses; in one of them, he, his wife, and child have a living room, bedrooms, study and kitchen, in another house it is just me and in the third house the maid lives. It is now only the beginning of May and yet the heat of the sun is already much higher than it would be in Switzerland at the height of summer. If it wasn't for the almost daily southern winds, which blow for a few hours, it would already be

An 1861 Galveston city view from the top of the Hendley Building. *Courtesy of the Rosenberg Library.*

almost unbearable. Between 9 a.m. and 3 p.m., there are almost no people in the streets, and if one is forced to go out during these times, one does not do so without the protection of an umbrella which shields you from the blazing sun. If the southern winds do not blow, then it is almost as hot in the shade as it is in the sun. The heat continues to rise until the end of August. This tropical, hot climate is responsible for the fact that Texas is so thinly populated. Not everyone can stand the conditions and many immigrants perish, due to the fact that they do not adjust their life style in accordance to the climate and are exposed to the elements too frequently. In Galveston every year in August, September and October the yellow fever arrives from the West Indies and New Orleans, and creates terrible ravages. Whenever this illness arrives, almost all connections of society are dissolved. During these times of isolation no school can be held. I will probably spend the time of the fever in the interior of the country, where the fever cannot reach. However, there are plenty of other dangers in the interior, for example the wild Indians, which are currently very hostile towards the Whites. But even

An 1861 Galveston city view looking south from the corner of Twentieth Street and the Strand. *Courtesy of the Rosenberg Library.*

if I stay in Galveston, I'm not afraid because, first, not everyone is infected by the fever and second, not everyone dies from it once they are infected (Brother Wendt and his wife have already had it), and third, I know the hand of my God will do well with me.

A true pleasure are the sea baths here in the Gulf of Mexico, which can be enjoyed without danger, as a row of sandbanks prevents sharks and other large animals from approaching the shore. But the hot climate brings also many other comforts, for example there are two harvests per year. Already last month, April, I often ate new potatoes, which had only been planted in February. Further, there are a large number of delicious fruits here, for example, pineapple, bananas, dates, figs, and oranges. On the mainland they grow mostly cotton and sugar. Coconuts are also brought in large quantities from the West Indies. The most magnificent flowers grow wild in the prairie, for example, cactus, sunflower, dahlias, geraniums and many others. On the other hand, there are also many unpleasant things, for example, poisonous snakes, like rattlesnakes, copper snakes and moccasin snakes. There are also large poisonous spiders. And, when swimming, porcupine fish can sting you dangerously, and enormous crabs have a terrible pinch. Further, there are many large and small ants, which at times crawl in droves into beds, and I have seen half-inch specimens. But, of all these things mosquitoes are the largest plague, and which have stung me terribly. One has to protect oneself at night with a net that is being placed over ones bed. These animals suck out the blood and every sting leaves a small, painful blister. A large grievance on our island is the lack of drinking water. Wells cannot be dug because the water is entirely salty and bitter, because it is from the ocean. Therefore, rainwater must be collected in large cisterns and if there is no rain for long periods of time, there are great hardships on the people. This is the case now. Since New Year's there was not a drop of rain and there are many people who have to pay more for drinking and cooking water than you would pay for milk. Just now there is a large cloud over our house. Everyone is hopefully looking up. It is very late at night and I have to come to an end. You are just about to get up because when it is 12 o'clock midnight here it is 7 a.m. where you are; when you are eating lunch, I'm thinking about getting up and when you have eaten dinner, I'm arriving home from school to have lunch. Just about when the sun has gone down in Switzerland, think about it, that is when the sun is directly over my head. Now, God's grace reaches so far, so far as the clouds go. God's grace reaches also to you and in you and in your son and brother. I send you greetings, wishes of grace and I beg your love and intercessions. Friedrich Gloor.

Also many warm regards to all friends, especially H. and Fr. Spreuerman, Maeglin, H. Rev. Legrand, H. Rev. Respinger, H. Spittler, H. Jaeger, H. Lepp, H. Stoecklin and others especially Theophil, C. Roth, H. Meister in the country orphanage along with the entire institution, Mr. Busch and family in Horgen, H. Rev. Ledderhose, H. Gysin and family in Inzl. The whole Chrischona Institute.

It would give me particular pleasure if Sister Henriette would be so good as to give this letter to the above close friends. I have promised so many friends that I will write, but it has not been until now that I have been able to. I send greetings to dear H. Busch, all friends in Brombach, Horgen and Steinen and Haegelberg Horzland especially the 3 teachers Rosleder, Obergsell and Troutman; also to H. Lehr, Haag, Heuttinger, H. Lehr Wendlin and wife, the Waelterlin and Weissling family.

I warmly ask all these friends to always remember me Friedrich Gloor. Greetings as well to dear Jakob Hunziker and Em. Huber and H. Rev. Huber.

❦

Friedrich struggles with loneliness and guilt from his past in this letter. It is his first year in Galveston, and he experiences the sweltering heat of a Texas August and swarms of mosquitoes, yet he finds joy in swimming in the Gulf of Mexico. His faith keeps him strong through the struggles.

Continuation of letter dated May 9, 1855

On the third and fourth pages of the same double sheet:

❦

My dear parents and siblings!

As early as the beginning of May I wrote my second letter to you, but for various reasons it was not sent, and I enclose my earlier letter with today's letter. In my inner circumstances little has changed since my first letter, but some important events have made a deep impression on my inner life. The first was a disease that suddenly seized me and drove me to the brink of death. On May 24th I was suddenly attacked by a terrible fever after a previous minor malaise. It was already dark and I was in my room. I lay down dressed on the bed and completely lost consciousness, which returned completely after four days. I would probably have died from the first terrible attack that night, but God graciously guarded me because nobody knew about my condition. Pastor Wendt was in a congregational meeting, his wife already in bed. But the maid, sleeping in a little house next to mine, awoke and listened to my rustling and fantasies. She called for Brother Wendt's wife and some neighbors, who were the doctor and his brother. The doctor recognized my condition as extremely dangerous. He drew my blood and made me lay on ice Mrs. Wendt brought in. But my illness, a high-grade fever, which also caused brain inflammation, and increased so much that on the third day, the day before Pentecost, the doctor who visited me four times a day gave up hope. As a last resort, he tried the mercury that saved my life with God's help. I quickly got better and was able to go back to church on the Sunday after Pentecost. The course of disease goes very fast here. You suddenly get sick, and you either die by the 5th or 8th day or get well soon. Rarely does an illness last longer than 12 days. The mercury I received attacked my body so much that I suffered for a long time from the consequences of it.

This crisis made a deep impression on my inner life. I would gladly have died, for I had the certainty that God has forgiven me of my sins, and will be merciful to me; but the thought of you and of what I still have to replace and make good here on earth, was hard on my heart at every free moment, and also occupied my mind in my wildest, feverish dreams. For this reason I often prayed to God that he would save my life, and contrary to all expectations He answered my and my friend's prayers.

For two months I have given daily private French lessons to a student. It pays me less than 20 francs a month. But I hope things will get better in the winter, because in the hot season, the schools have few students. The heat is so terrible now that in my writing desk the piece of sealing wax Jean gave me has melted down into a lump. For this reason I would ask you to seal your letters to me with two wafers instead of sealing wax. (Address: Fr. Gloor, school teacher, care of Rev. H. Wendt, Galveston Texas). Immediately after my illness, I was accepted as a member of a society known throughout North America and is called the Order of the Good Samaritan and Daughter of Samaria. The main purpose of this order is mutual love, faithfulness and hope against misfortune, especially in catching disease. Upon admission, one must first promise solemnly to abstain from all spirited drinks, from wine, beer and especially brandy. One must neither buy nor to sell them, and with all the strength and means permitted fight against the intake and dissemination of mental drinks. Once you have done this, you then receive the secrets of the Order, and the secret signs recognizing the members in all the states. Then you make the promise of mutual love and loyalty and to maintain the strictest secrecy about the secrets. Our lodge has its meeting every Thursday night, and everything is spoken in English, which helps me to keep learning the language. I will soon speak English as well as I do French. Brother Wendt is also a member.

On June 29, I was present at an execution. A man who had committed 5 murders and had been imprisoned for 1½ years was hanged here. He was very obstinate, rejected any spiritual assistance and yet showed the most terrible mortal fear. He still declared under the gallows that it was not right for him to be hanged, and that there were many among the spectators who deserved it more. He then began to ask the people that he should not be allowed to be hanged; and should be liberated. While he was still speaking, the rope was put around his neck, and before he had spoken further, the ground was torn away from his feet. In Switzerland such criminals are often

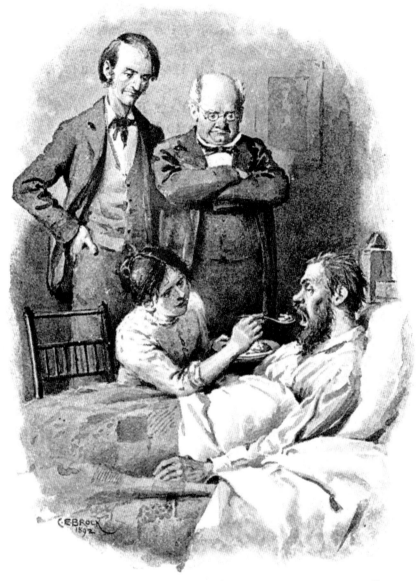

"SARY SAT DOWN BY THE BED, AN' FED THEM BEANS INTO BILL."

The yellow fever epidemic swept across the South, and home nursing care was often the only means of survival. Gloor suffered from and survived the deadly disease at least three times. *From iStock.com, Whitemay.*

In the mid-nineteenth century, justice in Galveston was typically carried out publically in the streets. *From iStock.com.*

dealt with in short order. Recently, a slave was accused of mistreating a white girl and killing her. The embittered people seized the accused murderer, and without trial and judge, he was laid on a pile of wood and burned alive. So it goes in the land of freedom! With freedom, it is not as much as you often believe. However, anyone can do whatever he wants, one is not bound by the narrow limits of decency. Here, one does not know so much about genius in Europe. The Pastor goes to the market with the meat basket on his arm or carries a piece of wood on his shoulder that he found on the way. Everyone can speak and write how and what they want, the people themselves choose their government and all officials, so to a certain extent they govern themselves. But the absurdity of shameful slavery casts a bad shadow on this so-called freedom. It was a sad sight when I saw for the first time in New Orleans a slave market where people, like horses, are placed for sale, where sometimes children are sold from their parents, the husband from the wife, and they will never see each other again. Here in Galveston too there are many slaves, and among them those who have a very bad time.

If only the climate was not so hot and unhealthy; I would want nothing more than to have all of you here. Father need not work more than outside to earn his bread, and fish the sea; which has fish taller than the tallest man and fatter than the fattest pig. Even some of the terrible sharks are caught every week. Also Brother Wendt and I sometimes fish in the Mexican Gulf. Mother would be able to earn a lot of money by washing. For every 12 pieces, be it shirts or stockings or dusters, you pay $1, and even then they will not be washed as well as mother can. Henriette could have the best accommodation here as a maid because she is a light-haired woman, as there is a great shortage of natives here to perform that work. Already the usual maids are given $6–10 a month including food, lodging and laundry. Jean would have to learn English first, and then he could earn $40 a month as a worker on a steamship. But I did not want to convince anyone to immigrate to Texas, because all immigrants have to fight much illness in the first years and the doctor house calls during the yellow fever period costs $5 and otherwise $2 for an office visit. (1 dollar is 5 Fr. 15ct.). Also, the voyage to Texas is something terribly difficult, especially if it is as long and dangerous as my 75 day voyage.

New Orleans now has the Yellow fever; so it will come here too. But the doctor assured me; I will either not get it or not get too weak, because I have already survived the climatic illness. Also, I believe that God did not save me from that illness to make me die in it. God will take care of me.

Now I ask you to finish all the greetings that I wrote on the first letter. Write me soon; the postage does not even cost 2 francs. You do not need the francs. Next autumn, some brothers from Chrischona may come to Texas again. But first write to me. I will remember you with heartfelt love and beg your forgiveness once again for everything.

THE TEXAS CULTURE

More Chrischona Missionaries Arrive and Gloor Writes of the Sin of His Past

In the next letter, Friedrich describes the first Tremont House (a Galveston hotel opened in 1839), which burned in 1865. The hotel was situated at the mid-dock of Post Office Street. The hotel was destroyed by fire, which nearly burned Friedrich's home as well, but his home was saved by his neighbors. The letter portrays Gloor's deep remorse for his long silence and expresses gratitude for forgiveness from family members. He speaks of the sin of his past but never identifies what events have haunted him throughout his life. Gloor reflects on personal growth since departing from home, attributing it to seeking mercy and forgiveness through God's grace. The letter provides insights into the daily life, experiences and challenges he faces in Galveston, while also emphasizing his spiritual journey and commitment to his faith.

Gloor speaks to the extreme heat, illnesses like dengue fever and the vigilance against the yellow fever epidemic. He also describes the peculiar customs and lifestyles of Americans in the South, including their casual attitudes and habits.

෴

Galveston, Texas, December 30, 1855[10]

To tell you about my experiences since my last letter I must go back to the month of August. For the entire summer since that serious illness, I was quite comfortable in the extreme heat. But there were many difficulties. The heat rose so high that one often did not know where to shelter from it, especially in the morning until 9 a.m. it was terribly hot until the cooling breeze would start. Often I could not sleep due to the heat for almost whole nights, and when I wanted to work in the evening, swarms of mosquitoes fell upon me, mauling me miserably, and they left me alone only when I lit my pipe and wrapped myself in the thick smoke of tobacco. Now that I am rid of the great plague, my blood has become so thin that I no longer feel the mosquito bites and no more swelling results from them.

May the Lord, our God and Savior, make each other blessed. I believe it, and I am of firm confidence and hope, that God will also forgive everything that I have spoiled with bold recklessness in my life as a sinner.

The Americans in the south are terribly weary people, and you would be amazed and laugh when you see the most distinguished people in their houses, in the inns, and even in the most educated societies lying around in positions that are considered immoral by us. If an American wants to sit comfortably he must have two chairs. He sits down on one chair then he puts his feet over the top of the back of the other chair so his feet are as high as his head. If he does not have a second chair, he sits next to a window and extends his legs out the open window. Here there is a large, distinguished guesthouse called the Tremont House. In the summer one often sees a pair of legs hang from each window of the three floors, so that it looks as if a shoemaker lived there, hanging his goods in front of the window. The ladies, who also want to make themselves comfortable, have armchairs made into swings, in which they often spend half the day sitting and half-lying.

For the summer I went out into the sea almost every day to bathe. The most beautiful place is the island's south coast, about 1 1/2 miles from the city. It is only recommended to swim here when the breeze blows, and when the waves break quite high and wild to the shore because otherwise all sorts of prickly fish, crabs and poisonous vermin approach the shore. Among the latter, is an especially dangerous animal known by the name Man-of-War. If I'm not mistaken, it is identified by the German naturalists to be of the genus nettle jellyfish. It is an exceedingly beautiful animal, the most beautiful sea-animal I have ever seen, in all its colors, about a hand tall, and with long red and blue arms. When these arms touch you, you feel such a burning

A SKETCH OF THE SEA SERPENT LATELY SEEN OFF GALVESTON

The Gulf of Mexico, while a relaxing respite for Gloor, was described as having many menacing creatures, such as this sea serpent off the coast of Galveston. *From iStock.com, Duncan1890.*

pain that you almost lose your senses. This happened to Brother Wendt last summer. While he was bathing, such an animal lay down on him and wrapped its arms over his chest and back, so that he was immobile with pain, and had to be carried out of the water and brought home. He was kept at home for three weeks with red streaks on his inflamed skin.

A FAREWELL TO CHRISCHONA BROTHERS

In 1856, new missionaries arrived in Galveston from St. Chrischona Seminary and were sent across Texas to serve.

The 1st of January 1856

I could not finish my letter yesterday because it's getting longer than I expected, so I sit down to write to you today, especially since today, on New Year's Day, I think of you more than ever, and you can put me in your midst more vividly than usual. God grant you mercy, peace and blessings in a new year! My dear parents and siblings, this is my heartfelt, greatest New Year's wish for you. And now I want to continue my narrative, where I stopped yesterday, for much more.

Sunday, the 9th of December was the day on which the public solemnity of our licensing or commissioning of the sermon or teaching ministry by Brother Wendt, President of the Texas Synod, was to take place. The church was festively decorated and garlanded. A large number of parishioners and other people had gathered. First Moedinger, one of the newcomers, delivered a message to the congregation, and then Wendt preached about John's words, "I am a voice of a preacher in the desert". He specifically emphasized in the sermon what a preacher in his congregation should be and what a teacher in his school should be, if he wants to do something good and enduring. Then the five preachers, then the two teachers, Dietrich and I, came before the altar, committed ourselves with heart and hands to the symbolic books of the Lutheran Church, and made the promise in the hands of the president, faithful to follow the pure doctrine of the Word of God and the evangelical faith. We promised to teach this in churches and in schools, and then we received the authority and were included in the Association of the Evangelical Lutheran Synod of Texas. The enjoyment of the Eucharist concluded the solemnity that has made an indelible impression on us all. The next day was also of great importance to us, as it was decided where each one of us should go. After a brief discussion and consultation it was determined that Moedinger should go to the state of Iowa, high in the north of America, over 2000 miles away; all the others remained in Texas; Beck went to Independence, Schag to Meyersville where Muller had died, Schumacher as preacher and teacher to Friedricksburg, Dietrich as a teacher first to New Braunfuls and then to San Antonio. I stayed in Galveston, according to my inner wish, and will stay here until the good Lord calls me to another place, since I have learned bitterly if you go away on your on initiative a job goes away and how hard it is to repent afterwards. I also love Brother Wendt, his family, many friends and the school children in Galveston so much that I could only leave with a heavy heart. For the time being Brother Kiekel stays here in Galveston, because the school has become too big for one teacher. We are planning to build a school at the east end of the city to serve many children from there who must now travel a long way to school. If this school does not come to fruition, Brother Kiesel will probably go further into the country after a few months.

The brothers left here the same week. The farewell saddened us; but we hope, if our Lord keeps us alive, at least once a year we will see each other again at the Synod Assembly. Moedinger traveled to New Orleans with the children's teacher, Jgfr. Munzenmeir, to visit his brother in New Orleans, Beck went to Houston and Schag, Schumacher and Dietrich to Indianola. So the brothers, who had come on one ship from across the world, left to the different parts of the new world on three different steamships.

Yes, I am getting sleepy; maybe tomorrow I'll have time to continue, so good night for now!

THE FIRST CHRISTMAS TREE
COMES TO GALVESTON

Friedrich celebrates the Christmas and New Year's holidays for the first time in Galveston and speaks to the introducing of the first Christmas tree to Galveston.

The 2nd of January 1856

It was very warm this morning; we had a storm at 7 a.m.; now however, the cold north wind has returned, so that one gets blue fingers. This rapid change in weather in this season is not only unpleasant, but injurious to the health. Almost all people feel uncomfortable today. I need to tell you how we spent the festive season here. The week before Holy Christmas we needed to prepare and we had our hands full, especially with preparations for a children's feast, which was to take place on Christmas Eve.

Only three years ago nothing was known here about children's baptism on the feast of Christ. Most Americans do not celebrate Christmas and the Germans soon adopt American customs, forgetting the sweet traditions of their homeland. Two years ago Brother Wendt came up with the idea of organizing a children's show. Since nobody knew anything about Christmas trees, he brought a tree from the country. The matter was so well received and applauded that the Christmas trees have now become a commodity here, and the steamships bring a lot of them to Galveston each year for the merchants to sell.

This typical Christmas tree was first introduced to Galveston by the Chrischona missionaries from Switzerland. *From iStock.com.*

This year a lot of gifts were donated for a children's party on Christmas Eve. We set up three large Christmas trees in the church, which we decorated the best we could with ribbons, wax candles, nuts, apples, and confections. The church was festively lit by a few hundred lights. After it became dark and the trees had been lit, we led around 200 children who had gathered in the schoolhouse next door into the church. After a lovely song by the children and a short, heartfelt address by Brother Wendt, the presents were divided among the children. They consisted of food and candy, books, writing materials, sewing kits, pocketknives, and the like. The cheerfulness evoked by the feast and the impression it made on both the children and the adults was all the greater as there were many children who did not enjoy Christmas with their parents. I too, was given generous gifts at home; I received from Brother Wendt a pair of black trousers, a hat and various other things I needed and from his brother-in-law, who loves me very much, a package of cigars which are as big a necessity as food due to the mosquitoes. Therefore, you must not scold me for smoking, for even Brother Kiesel, who never took up a cigar or pipe at Chrischona, found it necessary to smoke. Also, the tobacco is not expensive here as it is planted in large quantities.

Here, the week from Christmas to New Years is a special week of joy for the poor Negro slaves; this week they are completely free, can do whatever they want, and usually get a cash gift. Those who want to work are paid by their masters. The poor people are looking forward to this week more than our students are looking forward to the summer holidays.

The last night of the year is celebrated here just as yours. In some churches there was worship; with us until 10 p.m., with the Methodists even until 1 in the morning. On the ships in the harbor and in the streets of the city cannons and guns were fired with all kinds of folly. We went home from the church and stayed there, since we belonged to the temperance club, and therefore were not allowed to drink hippocras, to tea and chocolates, and we stayed together in serious talk and prayers until 1 in the morning. In accordance with the beautiful custom of the brotherhood, we selected bible readings for ourselves and our friends that night, and so I also selected readings for Henriette and some dear friends in and around Basel, which I will write down on the last page of this letter. On this occasion I ask Henriette to cut out the individual readings and deliver them to the dear friends mentioned. The readings for F. Trautmann, I. Brandlin, teacher Hauge, Rohleder and the youth club in Brombach, Mr. Bush in Haagen will bring good luck. You can give the reading for the dear friend Hunziker to Mr. Stocklin.

New Years day was festively celebrated here. Congratulations came from all sides, they were even printed. Whether they all came from the heart I do not know, but of many I do believe they did. On this day, especially the ships in the harbor were a beautiful sight. They had all raised their flags and pennants, which look very nice and festive, and this only happens on special

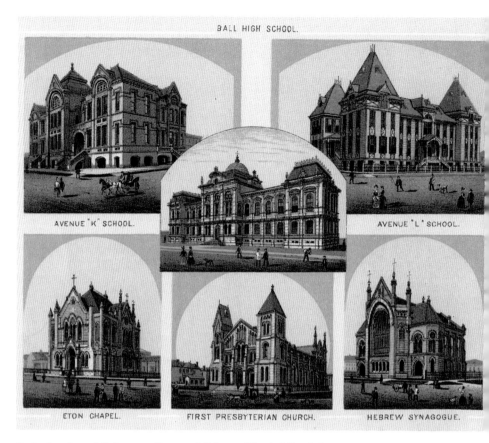

Early churches of Galveston. *Courtesy of Galveston Historical Foundation.*

occasions. The sailors of a large ship had asked for one of our Christmas trees, and they attached it to the top of the big center mast so that it could be seen from all over the city. Brother Wendt donated another Christmas tree to a Negro preacher who wanted to make his family happy. This Negro is a strange man. He himself is free and works during the week to earn a living. On Sundays he gathers a lot of slaves in an old hut and worships with them. His wife and children are slaves. This preacher cannot read or write, for here it is forbidden to teach a Negro to read. It is the intention of the slaveholders to keep the poor black race ignorant so as to be able to oppress and control them more easily.

I'm pretty much finished with what I really wanted to tell you, but as I do not like to send a whole page of blank paper to you. So, I want to tell you some more about the relationships of our church in Texas, of which

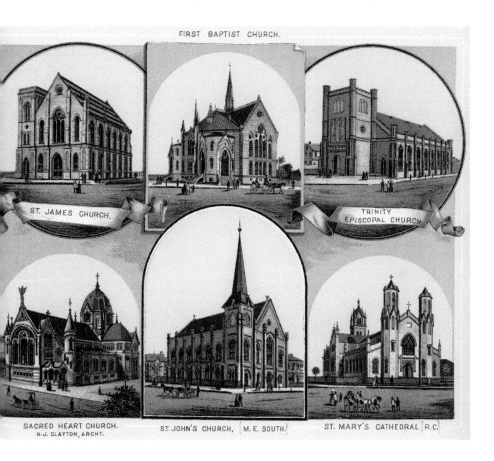

FIRST BAPTIST CHURCH.

ST. JAMES CHURCH.

TRINITY EPISCOPAL CHURCH.

SACRED HEART CHURCH.
N.J. CLAYTON, ARCHT.

ST. JOHN'S CHURCH, [M. E. SOUTH.]

ST. MARY'S CATHEDRAL [R.C.]

I believe will interest you and the friends who will be reading this letter. I implore you that you can tell me that I have told you some trivial little things, which may be of little interest to you. I have made it my intention to acquaint you as much as possible with all my experiences, so that you can put yourself completely in my position, and in my present way of thinking. Where I have said too little or too much, I ask you to understand my good, sincere will. Ask me about what you still want to know in your letters, for which I await with longing.

But with horror I notice that I was wrong, because I thought I had another blank page left. I cannot add another page; otherwise the letter's postage costs twice as much. So I have to close shortly, and say what would take many words with a few, and postpone the rest to my next letter. I so much wish Henriette was here; for, first of all, it is very necessary for Christian-minded people to come here to become a light to their surroundings. And secondly, she would do well here without having to exert too much effort, especially in

An 1861 view of Galveston Harbor as seen from the top of the Hendley Building. *Courtesy of the Rosenberg Library.*

the hot season. I therefore suggest you to consider that you could be much needed here and everyone that I have told about you wants you to come. But there is still time; you shouldn't come before the next autumn, as autumn is the best time of year. Think and discuss this with our dear parents. Write to me as soon as possible what you think about it; I'll pray every day until I again hear from you. Greetings to all who ask about me, especially to Rev. Legrand, Respinger, Huber, H. Spittler, the Fam.

…

Farewell all, farewell parents, farewell brother and sister / your Friedrich Gloor.

FINANCES, A PROMOTION AND AN OFFER FROM NEW ORLEANS

The next letter begins with Gloor expressing disappointment at not having received correspondence from his family and speculating about their well-being. He mentions his recent employment at a new school and the changes within the local German congregation regarding the school's structure and his own position. Initially considering a tempting job offer elsewhere, he ultimately decides to stay after the congregation improves the pastor's salary and appoints Gloor as the teacher at the first congregational school in Texas. Gloor discusses his financial situation, expressing gratitude for the opportunity to save money and send some to his family. He briefly mentions the possibility of studying theology in Gettysburg, Pennsylvania, but expresses uncertainty due to his calling to be a schoolmaster rather than a pastor. He reflects on the previous year's challenges and his gratitude for the support he has received. Gloor provides updates on his health, the extreme weather conditions in Texas and his longing for communication with his family.

Galveston, Texas April 25/26 1856[11]

I have already written to you that last winter this part of the country was unusually cold. One cannot remember a colder winter. It never snowed but on many mornings there was a thick layer of ice. You will say that it would not be dangerous if it were just thick ice. But try it once, come to Texas, spend a summer in this scorching heat and then see how it will freeze you in the winter even if there is no ice. I have frozen before, but never like this last winter. Clothes did not help, not even a wool blanket, which I threw over myself in the coldest days following the local custom. All the power of winter here is in the north winds, which are so piercing that the wooden houses let it in from all sides. Luckily the north wind seldom blows more than 3 days in a row and when it moves on, one gets hot days in the middle of winter. Only the months of January and February are consistently cold. March was already a true summer month. Everything begins to blossom; in April the potatoes, beans, peas and other vegetables were ripe and now, because of the great drought and heat, everything begins to rot.

The letter concludes with Gloor urging his sister to write soon, and he sends greetings to various acquaintances and family members.

CHURCH POLITICS
AND THE METHODISTS

Over the course of 1857, Friedrich describes the loss of his prior letters and yearns for letters from his family. He continues to seek forgiveness for his undisclosed former action—the guilt of it weighs heavily on him. We never discover the nature of what tortured him so over these years. He describes the day-to-day life in Galveston and his travels to central Texas, with vivid accounts of his experiences. He describes the Methodists as "bitter enemies."

Galveston, May 20, 1857

Cordial greetings, dear Parents and Siblings!!

First I must ask you to excuse and forgive me for leaving you without news from me for so long. I can assure you that the reason for that has nothing to do with you. Not a day goes by that I do not think of you with love. This past summer I wrote 2 detailed letters to you and the Stoecklin family. They, however, were lost on a steamship that sank between Galveston and New Orleans with everything on board. I postponed writing later from one week to another because I kept thinking I could send you more news or money. Then when my dear friend and Brother Wendt decided to travel home, I thought that he could give you verbally better, more exact and clearer news about me than you would get in my letters. As my dear sister writes, Brother Wendt arrived in good shape and has visited you and did my favor by reporting my essays to you. Isn't it true, he is a fine man and I am proud to be allowed to call him my friend. Yes, I can say my closest, dearest friend. From dear Henriette's letter I saw with regret that dear Mother has been sick and that in the recent past there has been a lot of sickness overall; that some of my friends with whom I grew up have gone to the better world. That gives me a lot to think about. Why has the dear God allowed me to be alive, even though I have earned it much less than these friends? Why did He once save me from near death; from dangers in which some stronger than I died? That is a thought which has concerned me since I last read Henriette's letter; God is to be thanked for His goodness and patience and to be asked that He daily give me strength and grace to stand every day prepared for death which must come sooner or later. That is true especially to one in a country like Texas, where death is near. Since Brother Wendt's departure I have been consistently healthy and in general all has gone well. Last winter, because of forthcoming hostilities, I firmly decided to leave Galveston and accept a new position; I notified the congregation but they did not release me and I did not want to force my will. To this end things were again rearranged to my satisfaction by the congregational body. And now I am completely happy that I allowed myself to be persuaded to stay here. I am again as now as glad and happy as ever to be here, especially since I am now more hopeful to be able to see my dear friend Wendt and his family again, with whom I have felt comfortable for so long and with whom I have experienced so many nice hours. And, I hope to experience many more. In my outward appearances there have been no great changes since Mr. Wendt's departure. Be so kind and tell Mr. Wendt I will write to him again soon. I take back the instruction that I mentioned in a previous letter because other thoughts have come to me. He will surely know about what I mean. Also, be so kind to also tell him Masers has moved to the North and I am now living with his brother-in-law V. Grahn [*postmaster*] on Mechanic Street [*corner of 22ⁿᵈ Street*] in A. Baldinger's house which is next to the location of a large fire last year. Unfortunately, I was not able to travel to the Synod councils. I deeply regret this.

Whatever part remains of my guilt, you can rest assured that I will destroy it with God's help. Until now I have not yet been able to do what I wish, because I have had many unexpected assignments, but be assured, I will not rest until this duty which hangs over me and has caused me many difficult hours has been fulfilled. And I am convinced that God will maintain my life and health until this happens. I thank you heartily for your patience and indulgence that you have shown with this matter and I ask you to maintain an even deeper love for me. In this letter I am not planning to write about my experiences last year and my current situations because you could have learned a lot from my previous letters to Mr. Busch and still more from the oral reports of Mr. Wendt. Now I want to tell you again that I feel good here in Galveston and have shoved the thought of leaving out of my head. Recently I was made aware of the possibility of going to Pennsylvania from a person I do not know personally. I rejected this possibility. The small irregularities in the community, which were not avoidable at the beginning of Mr. Wendt's absence, have been taken care of and everyone awaits with love and desire the return of this dear man. Mr. Ehinger is an industrious representative. I believe we could not have found a better person. We would have liked to have lived next door to one another but could not make that happen. Now we live about 15 minutes away from each other but get together every day. One does not yet know how things are going to be this summer with the health situation. The winter was very mild, in February there was already hot weather, but in March a cold north wind came again. Since then it has become hot and dry again and last night, after a long horrible dry spell, there was a wonderful thunderstorm. Mosquitoes attack everyone ferociously. We must cover our beds with nets and while I am writing this letter, I am smoking a pipe in order to keep the little pests at a distance.

Since last New Year's, a new role in the congregation has come to me, namely that of organist. We received a small organ from Germany that I play for community sing alongs. Because I never actually learned to play the organ, at the beginning I was very anxious about it and I always sat down at the nice instrument shaking. The first time went badly. Since then I have had a rather good practice on it, so that at least I do not have to fear getting stuck on a melody and the people enjoy the organ more and more. When you share this with Mr. Wendt he will be pleased. When I was at the state orphanage 6 years ago, without instruction, I began to play the organ. First in one part, then two, three and four parts. The dear Headmaster did not believe at that time that this exercise would ever be useful to me and he did not appreciate that I often practiced. However, I would now be greatly embarrassed if I had not at least learned the minimum then. Several months ago I began to learn to play the violin and Brother Ehinger and I often sing together with violin accompaniment so that we are not missing this enjoyment. Every Thursday evening we have singing practice in a Song Club, which we founded several weeks ago. We already have a nice number of members. Now and then on Sunday afternoons, which I have completely free, I go with Ehinger on horseback riding trips into the center of the island where we have friends all over the place who graciously receive us. We have also gone hunting together for ducks, woodchucks, and wild pigeons and we never come home empty handed. After Easter, Brother Ehinger went into the country about 140 miles from here, where the Synod meets. During his absence I had a very busy work schedule. During the week I had school, made visits, and on Sundays I had two Sunday school classes. In the morning was a class for Germans for which I am the officer with the prestigious title of superintendent. Afternoon's class is in an English Mission Sunday School, where I work as teacher; then morning and evening worship, so that on these Sunday evenings I was often so tired that I could not speak a word more. However, I always remained in good health during this time so that this summer is the first since I have been here where I am in the best of health and well-being. My friend Ehinger, however, who has only been here 5 months, often suffers from not being well; he still has to get through the difficult acclimation process which is already behind me. However, he has not been bedridden.

A short time ago another person from the Chrischona class, who came to Texas this past fall, came into our midst. His name is Tehr and since being in this country he has allowed himself to be torn from one business enterprise to another. First, he pushed aside a preacher in the community from his position rather than going to his appointed position. After several weeks he suddenly left the congregation, which called back the old pastor, and he became a shoemaker. Then he came to Galveston and got himself accepted by our most bitter enemies, the Methodists. He is now waiting for employment as a conversion assistant. The Methodist preachers value this position profusely because they encourage the mass conversion of people. They have a special pew in the church where one converts by laughing, crying, stomping, crying out, clapping hands and jumping around; this is called "to be converted lively to God". I ask that you share this writing with my dear friend Wendt and I would like to add here something that has special interest to him. The decisions of the Synod will be sent to him. He will not be satisfied with a lot of them. Also, Brother Ehinger and I do not agree with everything. Some things happened out of a lack of knowledge about different relationships and from critical, rash bias towards Brother Ehinger as a novice in Texas. So, they did not listen to Brother Ehinger and my letters arrived too late to be able to provide any information. I ask Brother Wendt to set all this aside and forgive the brothers their weaknesses and large mistakes. The dear God knows how to make things good again, what people in human incompleteness spoil.

The Brothers Beck and Fotisch stayed with us a while and have headed north. They traveled with Rev. Munzenmeier from New Orleans to St. Louis and have positions in the vicinity of St. Louis, as Lezterer so wrote to Roescher. Cheerful letters arrived from Brother Muckel from Gettysburg. In our congregation we collected $20.00 for him, which I sent last week to Mr. Anstaedt. Lezterer urges, in recent letters, that I should go to Gettysburg. However, I have with thanks temporarily declined his suggestions. Also, I have not been able to accept Muenzenmeier's suggestion to go to him in St Louis. I have decided to wait for Brother Wendt, whereas he will have a lot to decide. Brother Kiesel is in Wilton, Muscatine County, Iowa and often writes me friendly letters from the deep north. Just a few days ago I received a letter from the same cold state from Brother Blumer, in which he writes that he has been ordained by the congregational Synod and works in Grand View, Louise County, Iowa. Brother Maegle von Braunis is under a $2,500 fine because he is accused of a horrible crime with his students in Houston. He left the school where he was for 4 months and traveled to Comal City where a teacher was needed by the decision of the Synod. As far as I know he's innocent. Rev. Bohnenberger was not very friendly to you, my dear Brother Wendt! Brother Ehinger says that it was his influence that persuaded the brethren to take some of their unwise and unbrotherly resolutions. He and Brother Zizelmann seem to be angry with you, because you proposed one of the new brethren as preacher of our congregation instead of an old one. But it is my belief that none of the brethren in Texas is more able to stay and work here than Brother F. Ehinger, although almost everyone wishes that you might come back as soon as possible. [*Friedrich Gloor wrote the preceding shown in bold type in English so only Pastor Wendt could read it.*] In the hearts of most of our congregational members lives a warm love for our Wendt and I speak with almost one voice of the whole congregation, when I express this wish that he may soon return. So, dear Brother Wendt, hurry up, hurry up!! When I hear that your ship is coming into sight, every day I will go to a look-out place and look to the East, wide over the ocean, to see if there is not a ship with a red and white striped flag hoisted up and when I see it I will take the best horse from the old Burks Livery stable and gallop to the East End, but not into the horrible slime as I did when you departed; do you recall my telling you? I'm glad that you saw us then. We arrived 10 minutes too late to be able to call out our goodbyes for you to hear. When you return, pay attention when passing the lighthouse. A white towel is the sign by which we can recognize you and yours. Grant us God, that this reunion may be as joyful as I imagine and hope for! If only the yellow fever does not return. But even then we are lifted into God's hands. Stay safe, dear Brother Wendt with your dear family. Stay safe, dear parents and siblings. May God bless you all richly. Stay safe all my friends whom I cordially greet. Stay safe and think often of your Friedrich Gloor.

Galveston, May 20, 1857

My dear sister Henriette!

Many thanks for your dear letters, which are comforting for me, and encouraging and joyful every time. I'm sorry and I must be accused of negligence that I have waited so long to write. But for so long a time I received no answer to so many long letters that I wrote to you and Mr. Busch, that I nearly believed you began to forget me and that made me gloomy for hours, especially since my dear Brother Wendt is away. Now I am happy again since I have your dear letters in hand. I am always glad to see from your letters that you think of your distant brother with such true love and that a still higher, firmer bond connects us in our distant separation beyond the bond of blood kinship. You must believe me, dear sister, that my memory of you with inerasable characteristics is buried in my heart and that it is renewed through each of your letters. Our dear Brother Wendt knows how often and longingly I think of you. Oh, how pleased I am that you may see and speak with him. Ask him to tell you a lot about me. He knows me better and loves me truer and more sincerely than any other friend could love me. This is because I have also never been so open to a friend or value anyone more than he. Oh, that I could see him and you, dear sister, together. But it is how God wants it. I cannot advise you to act against our parents will. Just the opposite, with a bleeding heart I advise you: Stay with them, otherwise God's blessings could not stay with you. With dear Frau Wendt [*Mr. Wendt's wife*] you will find a joyful, true sister. If you could visit with her while she is in Basel, I would be uncommonly pleased. Do it, if you can. She will tell you some things about me, e.g. how I once helped to extinguish a large fire with my blanket, how I went to the market to buy meat, how I sometimes plagued her family when I was sick of their care, my moods plagued them and sometimes even annoyed them on healthy days, etc. Greetings from me to her a thousand times, and her lovely little Anna, who may still remember her uncle Gloor, and my dear little Elise, whom I probably will not recognize when they come back. You cannot believe, dear sister, how my heart clings to this dear family; I have never really known how much I love them until it was that I cannot see them every day. Brother Wendt's daguerreotype [*a photograph taken by an early photographic process employing an iodine-sensitized silvered plate and mercury vapor*] hangs over my own in my room, and I toss a long look at the two twenty times a day. I've set up his picture before me to hang so that I can see it all day. He gave it to me last Christmas.

As for your matter, dear sister, I am delighted that you are taking this course. Even if it is still dark—it will be light. Just hope, believe, and pray. And if it does not light up here—what harm? Then it is always a part of the body that can make you fine in the humility that is pleasing to God. My counsel is this: command the ways of the Lord! Let things go as they will and do not force steps there. But wherever you recognize the Lord's wink, you may act, but with caution and prudence, that is, with prayer. So much about that for now. It is commanded to the Lord.

I will conclude here, as I have already told the rest of the news in the letter to the dear parents, Jean and you. Only a small note to Brother Wendt; tell him I have gotten into a quarrel with the disgraceful Molling, whom Brother Wendt will get to know from the church messenger. This Methodist priest is becoming more and more cheeky and hostile; he hates Wendt, me and the whole Lutheran Church to the point of blood, and brings abuses against us in every record. Goodbye dear sister! God be with you! Greet all the dear friends and be hearty again and kissed by your dearly loving Fritz.

[At the head of the first page, written headfirst between the date and the title lines: *"Can you write me something about Karl Roth, it would make me very happy. I still love him with old love, but have not heard anything from him. Please, write back; I promise you a punctual answer."*]

[On the first page, parallel to the long edge, written in large script over the text: *"Greetings to you from my dear Brother Ehinger. He will also enclose a few lines."*]

GLOOR LEARNS TO RIDE A HORSE AND VACATIONS IN THE HILL COUNTRY

Friedrich takes a vacation by horseback through the Texas hill country, where he encounters friends and the beauty of nature.

Frelsburg, Colorado County, Texas, August 10, 1857

Dearly beloved parents and siblings!

You will already see from the title of this letter that I am currently not in Galveston, but on a long journey. Since I am having a rest day today, and have been thinking about you very vividly for some time now, and I wish to give you some news. I do not want to wait to write until returning to Galveston, which could be in about 3 weeks. So, I write to you from here, so that you get a letter from the interior of Texas. First, I want to tell you the reason of why I made this journey. The month of August is so horribly hot here that having school is hard to bear for teachers and children. Most children do not come to school this month. But this year I worked my way through without holidays. Because, despite the great summer fatigue about which everyone complains, my health was better than in the past two years. But it became necessary to thoroughly repair my schoolhouse. I was also advised, for the sake of my health, to give myself some exercise and a change of air for a month, and so I asked the community leaders to repair the building in August. Otherwise, I would have to take a vacation in a cooler month. In addition, a friend who lives not far from Houston offered me a riding horse to travel, so I accepted a short break for a vacation and took the steamship from Galveston to Houston, a city on the other side of the Gulf from Galveston on the mainland, on the 1st of August. From there I took the train, which now runs a distance of about 25 miles, to the friend from whom I received the horse.

You may wonder why I dare to travel on horseback. But here in Texas everyone has to learn how to ride a horse because you can hardly travel in any other way. I have ridden alone for more than 80 miles in these 10 days, and I still have a distance of over 130 miles ahead of me after which I hope to return happily with God's help. Despite the great heat that has already burned me brown, the healthy movement of riding is extremely powerful for me. From Spring Branch, where Pastor Haerdtle lives, and from whom I received the horse, I rode the first 20 miles through splendid corridors of majestic forests to the home of a friendly, hospitable American who kept me overnight. The next day I came to the Brazos, a beautiful river, which, as is the case with all the rivers of Texas, has no bridge built over it. For that reason I had to take myself and my horse on a boat across the river. A few hours later I found the house of a dear friend and brother, Pastor Tmolanek, from Bohemia, who has gathered a small scattered community close to the ruins of the old Spanish settlement of San Felipe de Austin. Here I stayed for 1½ days in the circle of the lovely family Tmolaneks, and then rode over many long miles of mountainous prairie where I saw no house and no man for a long time. Here I enjoyed the sight of some great herds of magnificent deer grazing peacefully around me. By moonlight I reached the settlement of Cat Spring where I stayed overnight with an American farmer. The next day I went through a huge forest in which I lost my way. As my horse started to get tired, I removed his saddle and let him graze in the trees. Meanwhile, I lay down in the shade of a walnut tree. It was about 2 p.m. and I put myself quite deeply in your midst. I calculated that it would be a little after 8 p.m. there, and thought that perhaps you were just sitting down to eat while I was still sheltering from the glowing rays of the sun. I wish you had seen me lying alone in the mighty forest, and that my horse was grazing so calmly about me, and he would sometimes look at me with his intelligent eyes.

After an hour I saddled my horse again and rode toward the setting sun until I came to a farm where I was again pointed to the right direction. The same day I reached Frelsburg, where one of my dearest friends whom I have

Gloor spent his vacations exploring the Texas prairie by horseback. *From iStock.com, James Gabbert.*

in Texas has lived for some years and works in a widely scattered community. As I unexpectedly arrived in the rectory of the dear Brother Roehm, I was received with great, warm joy. Here I decided to rest for about 6 to 8 days, and from there, accompanied by Brother Roehm, we made some excursions into the area. Brother Roehm preached yesterday morning in the little local church and in the afternoon we rode about 8 miles through a beautiful hilly area where on a farm about 30 Germans from the neighborhood had gathered. At Roehm's request, I gave a sermon on Luke 16, 1–12. I have decided that my horse and I will rest today. Tomorrow, I intend to ride as my dear friend's escort over the Colorado River to the settlement of Columbus, and next Friday my journey continues across the settlements of Industry, Brenham, Roundtop, Rock Island, Spring Creek and so on.

By the time you read this little letter, I will be back in Galveston with the help of God, and I will not fail to keep you informed. For today I have to close. Brother Wendt will probably not still be in Basel. But if he is still there, I ask you to treat him warmly, and tell him that I still long to see him again.

Forgive me for making it so short today. The oppressive heat makes writing almost impossible. Farewell, dear parents and brothers and sisters, farewell and love to yours, Mrs. Gloor. Greetings to all friends in and around Basel.

MORE ON THE VACATION
AND GLOOR IS "ENCOURAGED"
TO ATTEND SEMINARY

Galveston, February 22, 1858

Beloved parents and siblings!

It's been a long time since I last wrote to you, and I must first ask you to excuse my long silence. I have been so busy since my return from the past big vacation trip that I seldom have had a free half hour, and then I was usually not in the right mood to write. Even on Saturday's, when there is no school, I always have to make the most necessary visits from morning to evening, partly in the city with the parents of my schoolchildren, and partly on the island outside (the city), so that I only have Sunday afternoon to relax since I have Sunday school in the morning. Today is a holiday, the birthday of Washington, the liberator of the United States, and having just received a letter from sister Henriette a few weeks ago, I will use today's holiday to answer to you all.

As far as I remember, I last wrote to you from Frelsburg, Colorado County, where I had rest days on my vacation trip. At that time I promised you to write again, and as I have not kept my promise, I will tell you briefly how it has been since then. From Frelsburg, accompanied by my friend Roehm, I rode for a few miles over a large, hilly prairie to the northeast, in the direction of the settlement of Brenham, where Pastor Ebinger lives. I once visited him the year before last. Since no roads lead through this wilderness, I had to remember the direction exactly, and always look for horse and wagon tracks.

Therefore, I made slow progress, and soon after Brother Roehm left me, a terrible thunderstorm broke out. In a few minutes I was wet through. I had to get off the horse and walk it, shying away from the terrible thunderclap. There was no house to be seen far and wide, and it was not until darkness fell that I saw a light far off. Soon I came to an old log cabin where I was welcomed by a friendly American family. The people dried my clothes, gave me a splendid dinner, and let me sleep in their only bed while they lay down on freshly picked cotton. The next day I stayed there as I had contracted a violent attack of fever by getting wet. The fever passed quickly, and on the second morning I left my friends. The good people were so happy to have had a stranger in their lonely house that they did not want to accept anything from me. On the evening of the same day I came to Pastor Ebinger's house. He was having dinner with his wife and the doors and windows were open in the heat. I stuck my head in the window and wished a blessed meal. Both of them jumped in alarm and looked at me as if I were a ghost, because they had not expected that I would come 200 miles in the hottest season, and in this extraordinary heat. But a warm welcome came after the initial shock.

I stayed here a few days and nights in the company of Brother Ebinger and had some excursions into the beautiful, beautiful areas of the neighborhood. In these splendid regions many thousands, even millions of acres of the most beautiful land are left unused; there are no people to cultivate it. There are many square miles of prairies, even immense groves, into which occasionally a lonely traveler gets lost. In these places only deer, wolves, panthers, skunk animals, raccoons, pouch animals, snakes etc. live. Hundreds of thousands of people could live in this country without a lack of space. It makes a peculiar impression on one, if one compares this country with the European countries, where the people have hardly any space, and every patch of earth has to be cultivated very carefully so that everyone gets food. The land is also extremely cheap here. Many large landowners sometimes donate large pieces of land to deserving people, so that the land can be cultivated and inhabited. If someone settles on an uninhabited place and cultivates the land and pays a small fee, after five years the land is his property [*squatters' rights*]. In the first few years, such a settler would have a lot of trouble and suffer some hardships. He must first cultivate the soil, build a fence to keep the cattle out, then plant corn, sweet potatoes or bananas, a delicious fruit that is completely unknown in Europe, melons, etc. His cattle, which he lets freely roam the wide prairie without herding, provide him with meat and milk. If he finds a calf, he takes it home; then the cow comes to the calf every morning and evening and can be milked. What the farmer needs in terms of money for clothes, coffee, sugar, and such needs, which are very expensive here, he acquires from his cotton, which he plants each year. The children are not a burden here either, as is the case with some poor families in the cities, because the more children one has, the more cotton they can plant, since the children can help from the age of 6 almost as much as adults with the main work, which is cotton picking.

The market for cotton quickly grew in Galveston, and by 1858, there were more than twenty brokers on the island. Prior to the Civil War, there was no real need for an organized association of cotton buyers and sellers. Merchants bought cotton directly from growers at a mutually agreeable price and then resold it for a profit. The Exchange, built in 1878, sought to bring order to what was a highly speculative and often erratic cotton pricing system by providing a centralized trading office where people involved in the cotton business could obtain information about market conditions and prices.

Sketch of the 1878 Galveston Cotton Exchange Building, a center of commerce. *Courtesy of the Galveston and Texas History Center.*

Photograph of the Galveston Cotton Exchange Building. *Courtesy of the Galveston Historical Foundation.*

This year has been a very tough one for western Texas residents. As in the whole country, it hasn't rained there for 6 months, and only very little during the rest of the year, and the people hardly harvested any grain. So in the remote parts of the country, where it is very difficult to transport food, there is now a great shortage of money. A barrel of flour that weighs about 100 pounds costs $25 (or about 140 francs) in San Antonio, which is about 400 miles west of here. But this problem is the exception, and in ordinary years a farmer in Texas lives completely carefree and easy.

But I have already told you a lot about this. I want to get back to writing about relationships. In Brenham I found a young man whom I had seen before as a little boy in Basel. His name is Kuhe and he worked as a tailor at Mr. Wohnlich's, at the time we were still living on Gerbergasse in Mr. Alt Sel's house. Now he is a newspaper correspondent and rides around the country with books. He asked me to send a greeting to the current Mr. Siegrist Wohnlich, his former master, when I write to Basel again. I now pray to you to do this in my stead. He is married and lives with his wife and a small child in a lonely log house in the thick primeval forest. He is rarely at home, as he often travels for weeks, but his young wife told me that she enjoyed her loneliness. With this man I traveled about 20 miles to a settlement, Roundtop, where I met an old friend, and then returned to Brenham. On the way back from Brenham to Galveston I took a different route. Brother Ebinger accompanied me 25 miles to Buckhorns Point where we spent the night and then separated, probably never to see each other again on earth. The next day I rode through the Brazos River, which is usually done in boats, as there are no bridges. Due to the great drought, the river was so low that the ferryboats did not run, and I had been told that it was easy to go across in most places. So I confidently rode into the water, but suddenly, because I didn't know the low places, I got so deep that the horse had to swim and I had to kneel on top of the saddle to avoid getting soaked. But I got through very well, but because the bank is steep and high, I had to let the horse swim further down until I found a place where it could land and climb up. It was the first time I dared to go through a great river, and it will be the last time because I was terribly afraid doing it. I must consider it a special divine preservation that I got along safely. Then I was led away through the great Houston Prairie, the arduous part of the journey. It is an immense plain, overgrown with high grass, without a tree in whose shadow one could hide from the glowing sunlight. The water I brought with me in a hollow pumpkin was soon downed, and my poor horse and I were tormented by heat and burning thirst. For many miles there was no house; puddles had dried up, and besides, I did not know if I was riding in the right direction to reach the next house by evening. By noon, I came to a puddle that still contained some water but it was completely black, swarming with insects and so dirty that the thirsty horse did not even want to drink. I tried to swallow some from the stinking water, but had to spit it out. Then I unsaddled the horse and let it graze, while I laid myself in the grass and protected myself from the glowing sunlight with the saddle blanket. After half an hour, I got up again, and to my great joy, in the distance I saw a wagon covered with a cloth whose oxen were grazing, and next to it I saw smoke rising, a sign that an ox-driver was preparing his noonday meal. I took my pumpkin and followed the luring smoke. I found two very savage, benign, sun-kissed men, who greeted me harshly, but not unkindly. At my request for water they pointed me to a keg, from which I quenched my thirst for a long time and then filled my bottle. I did not accept the invitation to eat, but received information from the men about the way, and soon continued my journey. In the meantime, my horse was eating the grass, though nearly dead, the horse still had some strength and sap left. Towards evening I dismounted at the first house I had seen since 5 a.m. The next day I had a 4-hour ride to my old friend Woerner, where I and my tired horse rested from the strain of the journey. Four days later, in the beginning of September, I was back in Galveston and started my school again with new strength and good health. The air changes, the strength and movement, the healthy food strengthened me immensely, so that I have not been uncomfortable for an hour since returning.

Several times during the last summer and autumn, I received an urgent request from unknown friends in the north to come to the Gettysburg Seminary in the state of Pennsylvania and the Synod of that state asked me to come. If I came to study theology they would pay the costs. I do not know how that came about, since I never wished or expressed the desire to do this since I have been here, on the contrary, I am more of a believer that my current profession is the one instructed by God and the best for me. But I could not easily reject the beautiful, grateful offer. I therefore wrote to Brother Wendt, who also advised me to go. But I still had no certainty as to whether I ought to take the step or not, for there are many important reasons against it. The most important thing to me was that I still have obligations to you that I have yet to fulfill. Then the thought of having to live three more years on the benevolence of others was very difficult for me, for now, when God continues to keep me in good health, I can easily earn my own bread. Besides, it worries me now that I'm used to the southern, hot climate, and where I am so well situated, suddenly traveling 2,000 miles north to a country whose climate is even harsher than in Switzerland. This change is far more disadvantageous, like going from the north to the south. So I decided to wait at least until Pastor Wendt will be here again. Unfortunately, due to all kinds of circumstances, the situation has changed so that my dear friend and Brother Wendt, who certainly has become dear to you, does not come back but remains in the north and is now in Pennsylvania, almost half as far away from me as I am from you. The hope of seeing Wendt again was what made me want to stay here for so long. But I still had not agreed to go when, unexpectedly, in January I received an offer from a community school in New Orleans. I now accepted this offer, which I had previously turned down, as a sign of what I should do and decided to accept it. Therefore, I leave here at the end of January but I will have to stay here for three months from the day of termination if my replacement cannot be here before then. So I'll likely stay here until the beginning of May at the latest, and maybe travel to New Orleans in April, which city is about as far from here as Paris

Gloor explored the hill country of Texas on horseback, finding scarce water for both himself and his four-legged companion. *From iStock.com, Duncan1890.*

to Basel. You may be surprised that I have decided to go to this great city that I described to you earlier as so unhealthy. It is very unhealthy, and is visited every year by the terrible yellow fever, but that is mainly true for the newcomers. If you have spent some summers on the coast of Texas, and are acclimatized here, you can also endure the climate of Louisiana. Moreover, we are in the head of our Heavenly Father everywhere, and the yellow fever was as easy to find in Galveston as it was in New Orleans.

In terms of salary, I'm much better off in New Orleans than I've ever been, especially since food is much cheaper there than here. On the condition of the local school and other circumstances, the school board wrote to me in my appointment: The teacher at the German Lutheran Community School in New Orleans at the same time has to serve as organist of the community.

He has to teach at school all ordinary school subjects in German and English language. The average number of students is between 50 and 60. School is held five days a week, from Monday to Friday, 9 a.m. to midday, and from 1 p.m. to 3 p.m. in the afternoon. The rest of the time and Saturdays are free. The monthly salary is $45 (i.e., 240 francs), together with a free apartment. The community has bought a house for the teacher, which stands next to the schoolhouse. Food and laundry cost about 10 to 12 dollars per month.

The condition of the school is generally poor, both morally and physically, this is mainly due to the fact that in the past 3 years no competent teacher has been employed and therefore much has deteriorated. The congregation therefore desires to have a teacher whom they can expect to stay for a longer time. These conditions and circumstances are very advantageous and acceptable to me, although they were here also. The Galveston community does not want to let me go as nobody can make any significant objections about me. I hope that you too will not be dissatisfied that I take this step. It will also give me the opportunity to remit my debt to Mr. Siegrist and to you this year. I have now saved a small sum for this purpose but I have to wait to send it until I'm in New Orleans, because you cannot change dollars to Basel (francs) here. Hopefully it will be a bit more money then. I beg you, beloved parents and siblings, who have had so much patience, never believe that I will ever forget or neglect my obligations to you. I feel it more and more with each passing day, the great grief that I have already caused you, is still a heavy stone in my heart after this long time. It still often gives me bitter tears, although I am assured of your forgiveness, and I also know for certain that God has forgiven my troubled youthful sins. Until now, since I began a new life in this new part of the world, I have been saved from serious injury by many a severe temptation, and here I enjoy the love and respect of all those who know me. I also hope that soon your former love and confidence will return to me. God grant it!

I have to close for now. May this letter find you all in physical and spiritual health and well-being! All of you are heartily and deeply grateful to your Friedrich Gloor. / My next address will be: Mr. Fr. Gloor, / care of Rev. Ch. G. Moedinger, / No. 53, Port Street, New Orleans, La. / Please, write me soon! / Don't shorten your letters / Warm regards to all friends who still remember me.

THE TALE OF TWO SHIP CAPTAINS, THE HORRORS OF SLAVERY AND A BOY LOST TO A PRAIRIE FIRE

Friedrich recounts in explicit detail the horrific collision in the Gulf of Mexico between two steamships: the Galveston *and the* Opelousas. *The details of the collision and aftermath are recounted from the ship captains' testimony. Friedrich also recounts the horrors of slavery and death from life in the wilderness.*

Galveston, February 27, 1858

My dear, dear sister!

First of all I would like to thank you very much for your kind letter of the 9th of December last year, by which you have again quite pleased and encouraged me. I do not deserve that you write to me so much and so kindly and lovingly. For me to remain silent for half a year, as I have done, is really too much. When I read your letter to a dear friend of mine, Kersting, and came to the place where you write that you have been so eagerly awaiting the letter carrier every day for several months, and seeing him passing every day without a yellow letter. Then the kindly Mrs. Kersting seized your regret with passion, felt very sorry for you and scolded me for my negligence. Since then she has asked me every day whether I have yet written to you. I'll visit her tomorrow night and then I can finally calm her down and say "yes".

If you read these lines you will already have read the letter that I wrote to you all on the 22nd of February; but I hope you will not hate me if I answer your dear letter to you personally once again. That I should not see the dear Wendts and their friendly children again, I would certainly be quite sad. If I wanted to follow my carnal desires, I would be the councilor of Brother Wendt, who wrote to me from Pennsylvania on the 7th of January saying, "Do not wait any longer than until Easter, then come, rest with me and go to Gettysburg; there you are welcome. My wife says she is very much looking forward to hosting you in her new home." I would have loved to do that now but you will understand from my letters to our parents that there are many important reasons against it, and for a mere visit the travel is too far for me because even if 2000 miles or 7000 hours is not very much in America, it still costs time and money, and I have to save both since neither is mine.

You must have wondered a great deal about the fact that I want to leave the quiet, lovely Galveston on the beautiful shores of our gulf to the big, hot New Orleans, where so many thousands of newly immigrated Germans have found an early grave instead of a happy home. Do not let that scare you. That I go is not my own desire. I never sought for that place. It's been offered to me five times, and this time I've felt compelled to accept although I cannot go just now, as the New Orleans community wishes. I will stay here at least until the end of April. I am not afraid of the yellow fever; it is not as terrible as many people believe, and whoever is used to the southern climate either does not get it anymore or only slightly, but I ask you, dear sister, that in this respect you may remember me in your prayers.

Your story about your get-together with the Wendt family gave me a lot of pleasure. Others had much to tell me too, when we came back together! How gladly I would like to see the children again! Oh, so many times I have imagined how little Anna would jump up when she first sees me again, and shout, "Oh, Uncle Gloor, Uncle Gloor!" I wouldn't even recognize my Goddaughter, the friendly Elise. But this hope, like many others, has become water, and maybe years will pass before I see the lovely people again.

You urge me sometimes to speak Swiss German with Mr. Wendt, but I cannot do that anymore. Since the unfortunate Weber was here, of whom I have not heard of for a long time, I have not heard or spoken a word in this language. If I ever see you again, I would have to relearn, and I would certainly say "Jes" instead of "Ja" a hundred times a day. English has become much more familiar to me than Swiss German, and if I wanted to speak Swiss German, it would just come out as if you wanted to break standard German.

You wrote me about some sad events that took place in Europe last year. Likewise, there has been much sadness here since my last letter. The past summer was so dry that all the water puddles dried up, and on small Galveston Island over a thousand head of cattle perished of thirst. I watched it myself how at a bathhouse in the city more than twenty thirsty cows fought over leaking warm bathing water. Most cisterns were empty, and a small barrel of bad water cost 2–3 dollars. That was an emergency you cannot relate to. For half a year not a drop of rain fell and then, for a few months, only very, very, little. When I was at school with my children, a heavy thunderstorm started. It began to lightning and thunder. Everyone was happy; the people in the streets cheered and shouted merrily to each other: "Rain, rain!" Then some heavy drops fell, and suddenly everything was over. The clouds parted and the sun was burning hot again on the dry, glowing sand. That was a disappointment. Some children began to cry and I, like many others, could only fight back the tears with great difficulty. But when the emergency had risen to the highest, God had mercy on the thirsty people and animals, and sent us water in abundance. Yes, anyone who wants to learn that water is a precious gift of God should come to Texas in the summer! This winter has been unusually warm; the usual cold northern winds have so far failed, and we have consistently had warm, beautiful spring like weather.

The Galveston wharf in 1861, a hub of trade, as seen from the top of the Hendley Building. *Courtesy of the Rosenberg Library.*

A mid-nineteenth-century bird's-eye view of Galveston Harbor, as seen from the top of the Hendley Building. *Courtesy of the Rosenberg Library.*

Some time ago I was invited to spend the holiday season between Christmas and New Year's with the family of a friend who has settled about 50 miles from here in a nice area on the mainland. I left the day after Christmas on a steamboat, traveled over the beautiful bay of Galveston to the first landing place, from where I was picked up by a small boat. In this boat we drove almost all night up a magnificent estuary, on the shore of which lie the log cabin and the farm of my friend Nitsche. Here I spent the time with trips on the water, with very pleasant fishing and hunting. At times I went into the woods with my friend's son to shoot squirrels, which are eaten here as a great delicacy, and taste really good. Squirrels are different here than they are in Switzerland; they look grey and are bigger. We shot a lot of them. They are hunted because they do great damage to the maize fields. Sometimes we went by boat for wild ducks that teem there this time of year. I shot eighteen on a single day, which we mostly preserved. There are also fish from the largest and best species. I caught one that was so big and heavy that we had to hang it like a pig to scale it. In addition to logging and maize cultivation, hunting and fishing are Mr. Nitsche's only source of income. He leads a lonely but happy and contented life here with his wife, daughter and two brave sons. There are also bears and panthers in the neighborhood, but

you can imagine that I did not dare to hunt such with my friends. Before my departure the people asked me to visit them again, and if it is possible, I will do so. I wished that you could accompany me on such excursions. You would see and experience many beautiful, new and wonderful things that would astonish you, but that I cannot describe and tell.

Unfortunately, I have to tell you of another terrible, recent accident that took more than twenty lives. You probably have read what I wrote to Brother Wendt last summer about the terrible fire on the steamer 'Louisiana'; a misfortune that occurred on the 1st of June. As early as mid-November another steamboat set sail here from New Orleans. The saddest part is that this happened as a result of the most irresponsible carelessness of the captains and helmsmen. The large, beautiful steamboat 'Opelousas', with its many passengers and valuable cargo, sailed from New Orleans. At the same time the steamboat 'Galveston' left our harbor to go to New Orleans. In spite of the good weather, these two ships sailed into each other on the open sea on a clear, starry night, with such force that the 'Galveston' drove her bow into the midst of the unfortunate 'Opelousas' and split this ship in two so that it sank instantly. The 'Galveston', only slightly damaged, traveled a long distance and then laid anchor. Passengers' reports indicate that no effort was made by the 'Galveston' to save the unfortunate passengers of the sinking ship. From one of my acquaintances, who was traveling on the 'Galveston'

A typical steamship from the 1850s, the kind that would have come to the Galveston wharf. *From iStock.com, Ken Wiedermann.*

as a passenger, I have learned many details about the terrible event, much has become known also through leaflets and I therefore want to tell you about it in more detail. First, I want to translate the report of the captain of the sunk steamer, which he entered in the New Orleans court. Captain Ellis writes: "I left the Berwick's Bay on Sunday afternoon on the way to Galveston. At 4:15 pm I passed the lightship and 4 hours later I dropped the plummet and found 3½ threads of water. Immediately after, I found 7 threads and saw that we were over the shallows and safe in the water. That's why I now had to steer southwest against the Galveston sandbar. Around 11 o'clock at night it looked a bit foggy towards the land, but soon we had starry skies and only a slight fog on the horizon. I ordered a particularly bright light be hung about 15 feet high on the front mast in case the usual light went out. Then, before midnight, I made my usual round on the ship and found everything in order. The lifeboats were each equipped with three oars at their proper places. Thereupon I ordered the second helmsman to call me in case the wind turned north, and also advised him to look quite well for the 'Galveston' which, I suspected, had to be near us on its way to New Orleans. Then I lay down dressed on the bed and was soon notified by Mr. Jewell that they saw the 'Galveston' and that she was already very close. I jumped out of bed and saw the light of the 'Galveston' at a short distance and, believing we were passing beside her, I brought a green light to hang, but in the glow of that light I saw the 'Galveston' coming at us with full power. At that moment the helmsman shouted "hard on the starboard!" and while my ship turned to avoid it, the 'Galveston' drove into the side, about ten feet from the spot where I stood, and penetrated the center of the ship, breaking the steam pipe and wedging it tight. I immediately climbed onto the foredeck of the 'Galveston' to tie my poor ship to it so that the passengers could be rescued, but I saw no humans on the foredeck and when I felt the 'Galveston' moving backwards away from our ship, I jumped back onto the wreck, as I did not want to be stranded. I saw at first glance that my poor ship was lost, grabbed an ax, and tried to get to my passengers out of the cabins, the steam that came out of the broken boiler burned my lungs so that it was only with great effort I succeeded. I now found Mr. McFarlane busy with the big lifeboat in which there were already some women. I asked him if he wanted to take over this lifeboat, to which he exclaimed in a masculine tone: "Yes, yes, sir!" And he faithfully fulfilled his duty and lost his life saving others! I jumped to the other side of the steamer; but they had lowered the lifeboat and it lay upward on the water. I came to Mr. Fowler, the engineer, and the second helmsman and asked them and the nearest passengers to pull out the lifeboat; but when we got it, everyone jumped in. I got them out to get the lifeboat going first but the people scattered and jumped overboard in desperation. Those remaining were too weak to move the lifeboat. The water was now knee deep on the upper foredeck and I jumped forward to see if I could find any more people. I was followed by a woman. Alone, when I came to the wheelhouse I felt like everything was coming apart. I barely had time to grab a small canoe, about eight feet long, into which I put the woman and a passenger I found in the wheelhouse. Then a wave pushed us out. The small canoe threatened to turn over but I swam alongside and tried to keep it balanced the best I could. I saw several boats nearby, which I suspected belonged to the 'Galveston', and after some time one approached close to us, where several people clung to the outside. I saw a man hanging onto the lifeboat with one hand while holding onto a passed out woman with the other hand. I called to the people in the lifeboat to take the woman into the boat, but one of the boatmen said: "we have enough—no more!" But a sailor from my crew was in the lifeboat and when he heard my voice he ordered the others to take me and my two survivors into the boat. I then ordered the people to go straight to the 'Galveston' without me immediately, since the boat was already sufficiently loaded without me, and I jumped back into the water. I no longer wished to live at that moment. I saw several lifeboats pass by and since the screaming and wailing from the wreck had stopped, I hoped that most of my passengers would have been saved. My attempts to get back to the little canoe failed, but soon I was picked up by a boat and taken to the 'Galveston'. I saw one of my lifeboats near the ship, half full of water and called to my people. Two answered me, and the three of us immediately got into the boat, emptied it, and returned to the wreck. On the way we passed the wheelhouse that appeared to swim on the waves. One of the two sailors had injured his hand. I therefore took the helm and soon we met up with some lifeboats. In one of them, to my delight, I recognized Mr. Young, my pilot with two oarsmen; in the other my first and second helmsmen. I began to become sick as a result of the seawater I had swallowed and remember only a little more except that we were fishing for a drowned man until we came back to the 'Galveston' and were well received by their captain, Mr. Smith."

"If all the people had kept their senses no life would have been lost, for there were enough sailors who could swim at my ship to get 500 people to the water's surface, but people jumped overboard at the first fear. I saw two men shoot their pistols in despair and jump into the water. One drowned as he fought in vain to save himself on a floating barrel, which kept turning over when he made an attempt to climb it. The terrible roar of the escaping steam and the shouting of the unfortunate made it impossible to hear my orders, and the roaring of the waves in the ship and the crackling of the baffle frightened those who were unfamiliar with the terrors of the sea, so much so that they became quite numb. The 'Opelousas' had been built in New York only at the beginning of the year [*1857*], and since April 22, when I took command; I had only spent two nights on it. She was in the best condition. I was proud of her, as she was the fastest and best boat on the whole Gulf of Mexico. I saw how the first beam was laid, and I knew every plank in the whole construction. Her value was 100,000 dollars and the cargo was 70,000 dollars. At the sinking of the boat, 22 lives were lost."

So far is the report of Captain Ellis, as I have literally translated from English. The reports of various passenger eyewitnesses of both ships, however, give a somewhat different impression, from which, since I have already begun a whole arc, I want to communicate a few things to you. All passengers of both the 'Galveston' and the 'Opelousas' agree that the terrible collision was a result of gross negligence on both ship's officers, and that the loss of so many lives was due to a lack of discipline among both crews. Mr. Lyman, a passenger of the 'Galveston', relates: "I was a passenger on 'Galveston'. Sometime after 12 o'clock I was awakened by the crash of the collision. I hurried to the foredeck with my float, and found that one of our lifeboats was going to the help of the 'Opelousas' people, which was rapidly sinking. But this lifeboat was not manned by the sailors of the 'Galveston', but lowered and manned by passengers. The wind blew strongly and the sea rose up. The air was filled with the cries of the floating and the drowning. Several other 'Galveston' lifeboats were now lowered and spent about 3 hours picking up the surviving 'Opelousas' passengers. Meanwhile, the 'Galveston' had anchored about a quarter of a mile from the site of the accident. About one and a half hours before dawn the lifeboats all came back and were pulled up to the 'Galveston'. About half an hour later, two passengers floated past on a piece of wood. They screamed aloud for help but no lifeboat was sent to their aid and no effort was made to help them at all. At dawn, six other passengers were brought on board who had to cling to the wreckage for more than six hours, even though the 'Galveston', the main cause of the accident, was only a quarter of a mile off anchor. The rescued ones were stripped of their clothes on the pretext of drying them but some did not get them back, even though they turned to the ship's officers for help. Others were stealing their money and valuables that had stuck out of their pockets.

I had been on the canopy about an hour before the collision. There was not a human on the deck at this time except for the man keeping watch at the front. But I noticed that he slept as well. The lights were all burning. The sky was a bit cloudy, but the air was not foggy at all, and I think that people on the ships could see each other at a distance of over a mile."

Mr. Wood, one of the rescued of the 'Opelousas', tells in his report: "At about midnight I was awakened by a terrible crash and by the loud shouts of the passengers. I immediately jumped out of bed, went to the cabin, and asked for the cause of the noise. I got the answer that the boiler had a leak; but there is no danger. Nevertheless, I noticed great confusion and demand for floating belts. As such was in my room, I ran into the rear part of the cabin where I saw two lying on a table. Before I got to them, two ladies grabbed them and a man belonging to the ship's crew tried to rip one of them out of one ladies hand. I pushed the wretch away and told him the lady should have the belt. Then I ran out and saw what had happened; that the ship was quickly sinking. Just as I came to the door the water began to flow into the cabin. At this time, some passengers tried to lower a lifeboat. I climbed up to the top and the ship sank so fast that the water kept pace with me. There was a lot of confusion on the deck. Many broke off the benches and other woodwork to keep themselves afloat. I sat in a lifeboat lying on the deck, expecting it to become afloat when the ship sank. Some others came to me, including the Brave Mr. McFarland, who had previously knocked off the ship's railing. A powerful wave that struck the sinking ship drove us out into the water with the lifeboat. Here we pulled a number of people out of the water into the lifeboat and rowed over to the 'Galveston'. But now we noticed that the boat had a leak and quickly filled with water. We now had to bail the water with our hats and shoes. Mr. McFarland asked, "Men, if we survive, who among you will voluntarily go back to the 'Opelousas' with me to help even more?" A man answered, "I will!" But the water penetrated the boat faster than we could bail it, and when we were close to the 'Galveston', it went under. When it sank, two men held onto my feet. I involuntarily shook them off and soon returned to the water's surface. I did not see the brave McFarland again, but I could still hear his voice calling, "Let me go, I'm going down myself!" Looking around, I noticed a lifeboat floating on the water with its bottom up, holding a number of men. I swam towards it, and our combined efforts succeeded in righting the boat and getting in it. We had come a long distance when a large wave overturned our boat so we had to swim again. I was now exhausted but could get close enough to the 'Galveston' to grab a rope that I was thrown and was pulled onto the ship. Some others were saved the same way. We were greeted very warmly by the passengers of the 'Galveston'. My wet clothes were stripped off, and the passengers supplied me with their own; but I never got my own clothes back. Other survivors were similarly treated, and when we complained to the officers, they promised to help us regain our property; but this promise has never been fulfilled, and without the friendliness of the passengers, we would have landed naked."

From the story of another survivor I know I learned the following details: On the ship was the old, honorable General Hamilton [*former governor of South Carolina and mayor of Charleston*] in whose bedroom a floating belt was hung. But since his right hand was useless, he could not tie it himself, and therefore, he went into a cabin where he found a lady whom he asked for help. The lady replied that she had to fetch her child from the bedroom and not linger for a moment. The old man said with a smile, "Hurry, God help you and save your child; I'm an old man without much time left on earth." These were the last words of the venerable old man, who is now mourned by everyone.

A poor man from Alabama who wanted to settle in Texas was among the rescued. He wept for the loss of his wife and small child who had been torn away from his side by a wave. Five hours later, the two were brought aboard the 'Galveston' alive to the delight of the man. The woman had clung to a piece of wood, and a man who had rescued himself on the same piece of wood told the woman that she held onto his hand for five hours while she and the man were trying to hold the child above the water even though they were barely capable of holding each other, yet they endeavored to breastfeed the crying child. This was also her first business when she was brought to the 'Galveston' and her husband welcomed her with joyous tears. Motherly love had been the only feeling that filled her in her terrible situation. The rescued were brought to New Orleans, and found the friendliest reception. They were provided with clothes and linen, and the owner of a large hotel took them all in and told them that they could stay without paying a dime until they were able to continue their journey. A criminal proceeding was ordered over the captain's and helmsmen's actions which are not yet completed, but they are expected to be sentenced to long prison terms.

You do not have to tell me, dear sister, that the detailed narration of the terrible misfortune makes my letter so long. At first, I did not want to write so much about it, and only now do I see that it's turned into five pages long. When reading it you shouldn't run out of patience. You will get a sense of how little human life is respected here in America. I believe that some who travel to America, or any such a journey so recklessly would think more seriously about the matter and would be driven more into prayer if they could witness such scenes. I will make the journey to New Orleans in a few weeks, perhaps just at the time you read this letter, and though I am well preserved in the hands of my Heavenly Father, it is my serious thought that in this way, in the short time of my being here, four ships have perished, of which I have seen one, the unfortunate 'Louisiana' perish.

But enough for this time on shipwrecks, which are unfortunately so often an occurring thing that almost every newspaper finds newly displayed. I want to notify you of other incidents that may interest you, because I still have time and space left.

Yesterday a Negress, who had murdered her mistress, was hung here. The poor woman had been sold away from her children, and she fell into the possession of an inhumane woman who kept an inn here. The slave girl was treated very cruelly. Among other mistreatment, an iron-spiked collar was put on her so that she should keep her head straight. Driven to despair by this treatment, when she was alone in the kitchen with her mistress, she seized an ax, and killed her mistress, and threw the corpse into the cistern. She was soon discovered; they made the poor woman a short process, and hung her up. That is the curse of slavery!

Sometime ago there was a woman in our house whose sad life leads me to tell you something. I first met her and her husband in the summer before

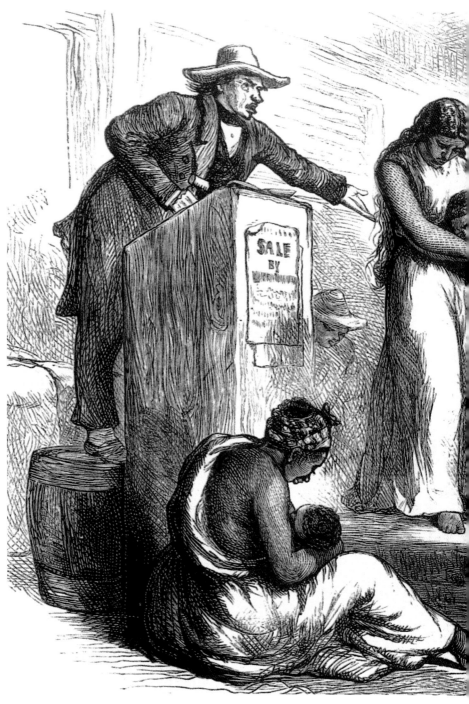

Gloor viewed slavery with great criticism and would have witnessed such a typical auction.
From iStock.com, Duncan1890.

last. At that time they lived at the Colorado River, where I visited them on my way back from my journey there. Since a Negro conspiracy had broken out in that part of Texas, travel was unsafe, so I had to stay with them for a few days and I became acquainted with them. At that time the Negros had conspired to kill all white men in that district, but fortunately the conspiracy was discovered before the complete outbreak and the leaders were sometimes hanged and sometimes whipped to death. When calm was restored I continued my journey but visited those people again last summer. Just before my second visit they had lost a son in a terrible way. One evening, the father told me, that a neighbor rode up to him, telling him that the prairie was in flames all around and that in a short time the fire would reach his farm. You have already read about the terrors of a prairie fire; therefore, I only want to remark here that if one is surprised by such a fire, only one means remains to save oneself, if one does not have time to escape the threatening elements on a good horse. Where one lives, the dry grass is cut down so that when the big fire approaches, it can no longer find any fuel. That's what the man did. He lit the prairie at various points around his farm, and then quietly returned to the house. But he missed his little boy. He went out to look for him and found him lying by the fence burned. The child had gone after his father unnoticed and had found his death in the fire set by his father.

A few months ago, this hard-tested man sold his farm to move north with his wife and the remaining two children. They stayed with us for a few days while passing through. One week later, one morning, the wife with the two children suddenly came back to us and told us with tears that her husband had died on the steamboat and that they were heading back to their former home. The poor woman herself was so ill that she had to stay with us for several weeks before she was able to continue her journey. This is just an example of the suffering lives of some American settlers. If all the similar cases that occur in this country on a daily basis became known, books could be focused on stories of these most terrible tales of suffering and tragedy.

Well dear sister, I must hurry and come to the end. I am grateful for your many messages from the old homeland. Some dear memories have awakened in me again. I was very pleased with what you told me about my former friends, Karl Roth, J. Hunziker, etc. I very much wish to have the opportunity to get in touch with Karl Roth. We knew and loved each other from our earliest youth, and it often hurts me that we have been so cold for years now. Why do you not write to me about my dear friend Theophil Stocklin? I very much want to know more about him and the whole dear family very soon. Your question regarding Brother Maier in New Orleans

I can briefly answer here. He has taken on the church where Brother Muenzenmeier used to be preacher. When I arrived in New Orleans three years ago, I visited Brother Muenzenmeier first, but I had to wander around in the big city for a whole day until I found him. The first night I spent on the American mainland I slept in a bed with Brother Muenzenmeier. At that time I was so weakened by starvation and deprivation from the long sea voyage that I thought I could not live much longer. And yet, Brother Muenzenmeier, who at the time was healthy and strong, had already passed into eternity half a year ago, while I, by the grace of God, was still alive and since that time have gained health and strength every year. A few months before his death, Brother Muenzenmeier left the community to move to the northwest, and Brother Maier, who was then in New Orleans at that time, was elected in his place. The community belongs to the Presbyterian Church which is much like the Reformed Church. Their confession, since they are not strict Calvinists, is not at all different from that of our Reformed churches in Switzerland, and the sister of Brother Maier can be perfectly calm in this regard. The situation here means that every congregation joins a church community without the inner life of the individual congregation members having to undergo a change. We find devout, pious men in each of the many church communities, but there are hypocrites in every one. Most of all, however, among the Methodists. As for Brother Maier, I believe that as a Presbyterian preacher, he is the same Brother Maier that would become a Lutheran preacher. The name (Presbyterian) does not make us happy, but the faith, whether we are called Paulish or Kephish or Apollisch. I am looking forward to seeing my dear brother again soon, although unfortunately I will live far away from him. Say this to sister Maier, and be so good, and greet her warmly.

Well, dear sister, I have written you a long letter, and I think you will have much trouble reading it and become quite impatient. It would be nice if you wrote me soon an even longer letter as a punishment; if we weren't allowed to repay evil with evil I would gladly forgive you for such revenge.

...

Write me right back under the address. By closed mail / Mr. Fr. Gloor, care of Rev. G. Moedinger, New Orleans / La. / Do not postage your letters anymore! / Do you hear!!

YELLOW FEVER NEARLY TAKES FRIEDRICH'S LIFE

Friedrich travels to New Orleans briefly for a new job. He describes the devastation of yellow fever. Yellow fever was a fatal disease resulting in a gruesome death for many in southern populations. The disease, which was carried by mosquitoes, made the hot, humid climate of cities like New Orleans and Galveston particularly deadly and prone to spreading the disease.

February 4, 1859 Galveston, Texas

Dearly beloved mother, brother, and sister!

Half an hour ago Brother Ehinger brought me your letter, sister Henriette, which was forwarded to me from New Orleans. As much as I rejoice every time I receive a few lines from you, beloved ones, this one initially amazed me. I find on the first page reproaches that I am not writing, and these reproaches would certainly be the fairest that have ever been made if I had really not written since I recovered by God's grace from the yellow fever. But I wrote, and I can hardly believe that the letter I wrote in November may have been lost, since the letters are now so safe when there is no shipwreck. There are also things in your letter that show I wrote to you, for example that I was called back to Galveston, and that I would like to return there and get away in general, if I could find a good successor for my place in New Orleans. If you had not received my letter, how do you know then, dear sister, that I had the yellow fever to such a high degree and that I got well, so that I could start school again? [*There was no November 1858 letter included in the collection, which suggest that Friedrich's letter was never received by his family.*] Brother Ehinger tells me that he had written to Basel that I would probably come back to Galveston, but he does not believe that his New Year letter has arrived. Please, explain this riddle to me. I wrote that letter, if I remember rightly, towards the end of November, when Brother Moedinger read a few passages from it, then I included a reply to sister Caroline Meyer's letter, and addressed the whole thing as I would address any letter. Maybe it got stuck somewhere, and you have received it since. If it's lost, I am all the more sorry for the fact because there is a question in which I desperately wish to receive an answer. In case it is really lost, I will briefly repeat its main content here.

As you already know, in April of last year I followed a call from Brother Moedinger's congregation in New Orleans. Saying goodbye to my dear friends in Galveston, especially the children, hurt me unspeakably. On a Sunday I said goodbye to the community and children. The children cried so that no words could be spoken anymore and no one's eyes remained dry. Also, I could not soon stop thinking about crying myself. If I still had been able to take my word back to go to New Orleans I would have been weak enough to do it. But my successor was already in Galveston; I was expected in New Orleans; I had to go. I would leave on Thursday. On Wednesday evening, all 60 school children came to our house, sang a farewell song, and handed me a large number of small gifts to remember. I have never forgotten the love and attachment with these children. When the ship sailed out into the Gulf, and dear Galveston disappeared bit by bit into the distance, it seemed to me as if I had lost a whole world, and I had to go into my little cabin to hide my tears from the other passengers.

I almost met another accident. I had my luggage brought to the ship on Thursday, but on my way to the harbor I was stopped so many times by acquaintances that I was too late. The ship was already offshore and leaving with my things but without me. Luckily another ship left the next day and after many inquiries and searches in New Orleans, I found my luggage again. My crossing to New Orleans was pleasant; but I found some things there differently than I had expected. Although I was received with love and joy, I found the school in such a terribly overgrown condition that I almost wanted to lose my courage. I enjoyed much love and friendship in dealing with the brothers Moedinger and Meyer, but my health, which had been very good in the last two years in Galveston, was greatly affected by the change. The climate in New Orleans is much hotter and unhealthier than Galveston, where in the hottest summer there is always a cool north wind blowing. I was suffering all summer long, even before the yellow fever broke out. It was difficult for me to get used to the urban cold of the city because I had for a time been living the quiet and cheerful life in Galveston. Finally, the yellow fever came and pulled away dear brother Meyer so fast. That was a hard blow for me. I had loved him so much, and the whole week I was always looking forward to the Sunday nights we usually spent together. With Brother Meyer dead the hardest time began. Thousands were swept away, and in a single day 115 dead were listed, not including those who went unnoticed. Each week 600 to 700 deaths were being reported. Almost every house was experiencing dying, and the fever did not spare even those who had been born in the city. I also suffered the pain of losing some of my schoolchildren to the fever. In September Brother Moedinger caught the disease. We feared for his life, but while whole households died on both sides of us, he was kept alive. He was still weak from the ill-conceived disease when on a Sunday morning, September 26, a man came to him whose wife fell ill with the fever and wished that somebody might pray with her. Brother Moedinger was not yet allowed to go out, and sent the man to me with the request that I go with him instead. The man told me that his wife was not breaking black, but surely she was going to die. They lived in a remote part of the city, and we had a long way to travel in the heat of the day. When we entered the room the woman lay there covered in black blood. It was a horrible sight. She had broken black while we were on the way there and died a few minutes after our entrance. Although I had seen many fevers and had seen people break black without damage, in this case I was not prepared for such a gruesome sight. A shudder seized me, and on the way home I felt as if the fever had seized me as well. But I kept school the next day, though I already felt pain in my back and limbs. In the night of the 27th to the 28th of September I could not sleep; I had a headache, but got up in the morning because I always thought it might just be temporary malaise, as I often had last summer. I especially believed this because I still had an appetite. But when I sat down to breakfast, an indescribable disgust came over me. I went to school, but already in the first quarter of an hour the fever shook me. The children looked at me restlessly and they yelled, "The teacher has got the fever!" Of course, I felt that too well myself. I dismissed the children and went to Brother Moedinger, who was frightened at my sight and immediately brought me to bed, gave me a hot footbath and the first remedies, and then sent for the doctor. He soon came and brought with him an experienced, faithful nurse, who cared for me during the whole duration of my illness and the lengthy convalescence with motherly care day and night. The leaders of the congregation and other friends, of who were always present, shared in the night watches. Of the first three days of my illness I know little, though I never lost consciousness, except on the fifth night. I did not feel much pain, except on the first day, when the headache and back pain are always the worst. I constantly had to have ice on my head, stomach, and in my mouth day and night. I also had ice water to drink as often as I wanted. On the third day the fever subsided, and on the fourth day I felt so well that no one thought of danger except the doctor and the nurse. Despite the doctor's ban, many visitors came on Friday and I was able to speak to them quite well and without complaint. But that night the fever suddenly returned with a terrible violence. An indescribable weariness, nausea and pain in the stomach seized me. I felt a worry that I would break black but I was too weak to say anything. At 10 p.m., before the doctor could be summoned, the first bumps, which were associated with such cramps and pain, broke such that I almost lost consciousness. I was told later that this spasmodic thrust had lasted over three hours, and that everyone expected my death. The nurse put ice on my skin and in my mouth, which was filled with blood, and the doctor stayed with me all night. By morning my consciousness returned but I was unable to receive the Eucharist. Brother Moedinger afterwards told me that in the night my pulse and breath had suddenly ceased, and that the nurse jumped and shouted to him that I was dying. Two days later I was still in great danger but against all expectations, the Lord once again spared my life and made it better with me. For a long time I remained so weak that I could not move, and the vomiting occurred twice more, though not as strong as the first time. When I was allowed to enjoy some tea and chicken broth again I had everything, mixed with blood, break out again, so I had to taste a few drops of brandy every few hours to settle my sinking feeling. But this condition stopped and I was allowed to gradually enjoy more substantial food. On the 15th of October I was already able to leave the room on two crutches and was picked up by my host in a chaise. My recovery was regarded everywhere as a true miracle, as it is in my eyes also. Never before had death been so close to me, and very few who were so close to him (Brother Moedinger) at that time now still enjoy their lives. When I met Brother Moedinger we had to praise the grace and goodness of the Lord who had left us in the midst of plague and death. I do not know what purpose led the Lord to save me again from near death, but I know that it was for a good, wholesome purpose. I renew to him my life and all his powers, and ask him that he will fulfill his purpose in me!

Also in my dear Galveston the yellow fever had arrived. From there I received over 30 letters in a short time, so I became acquainted with everything that was going on. The fever started in Galveston a few weeks later than in New Orleans and did not rage as much. But I also have to mourn the deaths of 5 of my dear schoolchildren, some Sunday students, two other children, and a large number of dear friends and acquaintances. Brother Ehinger continued to perform his duties day and night to the sick at deathbeds but he was miraculously spared. But the hardest and heaviest blow was still ahead of me. It was the death notice of our dear father that I was lucky at one time to have. [*The continuation of the letter is missing.*]

[*On the first page, parallel to the long edge, written in large script over the text:* "Greetings from / my old acquaintance Fried. Ehinger / also Mr. Gysin."]

THE CONGREGATION REQUIRES THAT GLOOR MUST FIND A WIFE

Returning to Galveston, Friedrich is pressured to take on a wife. In these next letters, first he seeks his sister's help in finding a wife from Basel. But finding a potential bride in Texas, he later seeks his sister's blessing of marriage. He also speaks to church politics and congregational division.

May 28, 1859 Galveston, Texas

My dear, dear sister!

Actually, I should now also begin this letter as yours usually begin, namely with a rough reference that you answer my question. But I will refrain from doing so, and hope that in the future you will imitate my current good example and answer my letters quickly and punctually. Your last letter, dear sister, has been a great pleasure to me, although it does not contain much pleasant news. But again, he was a sign of life and love, and as such he [*assumed to be Friedrich's father*] was dear and welcoming to me. I was particularly distressed to hear that in vain was I looking forward to having my dear mother and you with me. It is very difficult for me to realize the fact that I should never see you, dear ones, again in this life. The Lord certainly knows why he does not fulfill this beautiful hope, but it will be difficult for me to submit completely to His will.

Since my being here the Lord has provided me with health and all necessities. Already in the first month, when I returned to Galveston, so many children flocked in that the schoolhouse could not hold all, and I needed to reject some. Last month I had 75 students. Now the number is decreasing a little because the little ones cannot come to school during the already prevailing summer heat. Through the abundant income that I had earned, I was able to fully re-establish myself here, and I have friends sending you something to repay my debt. I ask our Jean to write to me how I stand now with Mr. Siegrist, and whether I can count on it soon, so that my small savings will benefit mother. Through Brother Wendt I sent $25.— the last time $15.—and now again $15; that's $55, or 275 francs. The fact that it is so little is partly due to my illnesses, especially the last one, which cost me more than $100, of which I have paid thirty dollars since I arrived, partly due to the fact that I did nothing in the first year, I earned a little in the second, and I needed that money to get clothes, laundry, etc. which I had run out of on the trip and in the first year of my being here. It is only since I have mastered the English language and the local school method that I have become known among the people, and have enjoyed a significant salary. Because so many people come to this country, one must be exposed to distrust from the people for years before one wins their full confidence. By the grace of God, the latter has been fully in my favor here and in New Orleans. I now compare my position and the love and respect that is shown to me almost on all sides with my earlier life and I must praise and break out thanks for the forgiving grace of God. It is just so humbling for me that I find nothing in myself through which I have earned all this good, and must attribute everything to the mercy of the Lord. Oh how good and gracious the Lord has been to me, that he did not throw me away, as I deserved with my sins, but led the consequences of my aberrations in such a way that I was led into this country and into a sphere of activity where I can work for his kingdom and be useful by his grace. Here I do have a place as a link to human society, while I was a burden to it outside. Praise and thanks to Him for his patience!

Dear sister! I must now come to a very important matter for me, which I would like to advise you. My position as a community teacher, which brings me together with all kinds of people and makes the topic of conversation of many people definitely requires, quite well, that I should soon set up my own home. If mother and you could have decided [*to come to Galveston*] this would have been the easiest way for a long time. We would have formed a small family together and I would have had my home, that I need so much now after years of wandering around with strangers. Since you cannot come now, I must get married. I cannot possibly give you all the reasons that make it necessary for me. But you will believe me when I tell you that it is necessary for me and that I have been required to do so from all sides. In New Orleans this was even more the case. If I stayed there, perhaps I would already have been married. My successor in New Orleans is now married after scarcely being there a quarter of a year. My salary and other circumstances are such that a modest family can live decently and without any worries. Next month the congregation will confirm the salary that certain ministers have set, which will average $50 a month, not including what I earn by private lessons in the winter. The expenses of a small family are only slightly higher, often not even as high as a single man who has to pay dearly for every small thing. In this respect, if the Lord continues to give me health and life, I would be perfectly taken care of. But the most important question is still: From where should I get a partner? Here in Galveston as in New Orleans, I know many girls, including some who would not answer "No" to an inquiry. But among all those whom I have met here so far, none are one with whom I believe would be a support and help in all relationships and a true companion on the path to eternal life. And though neither my stand in general nor my person in particular are very demanding in terms of secular education and knowledge, the most necessary aspects of them should still be known, and girls brought up here or immigrated here are almost completely lacking. Therefore, I would like to ask you, my dear, only sister, to assist me with friendly, sisterly advice, and to bring this concern of mine to the Lord. In such an important matter I would not take a step in it if it were not finally, absolutely necessary. There is still time until the end of this year or the beginning of next year. I beg you, dear sister, to convey my request to dear Mr. Gysin and Herr Spittler, possibly also to M. Pfr. Legrand, and to offer me their basic advice. Further, I ask you to write to me, if you know among your acquaintances a dear, believing soul of whom you are convinced would not only possess the requisite qualities, but could also decide to make the long journey to a foreign country in order to meet and connect with a simple community school teacher. I do not want to tell you what further thoughts I have about it because I believe that they will be revealed to you if they are from the Lord. But do not write or do anything without discussing it with the experienced, believing fathers I have named above, and with our dear mother and Jean, and be as open to them and to me as I am to you. Dear Mr. Spittler and Mr. Rev. Legrand, with their local relationships, and with all that their public positions are certainly well known. They will certainly recognize the necessity and some of the reasons that prompt me to take this step without my describing them here. Perhaps you will say that I should leave the Lord alone, that when the time comes He will bring me a life companion. I also have this faith and confidence; yet I also know that it is not part of God's order that we should be weary and inactive. Rather that we should act according to His will, which he gives us in many ways, also through the external circumstances in which He places us, announces and reveals. Write me very soon about it so that I can get to know your thoughts on this matter. In general, I would like to ask you to answer my letters soon, and I promise to wait no more than a week to answer yours. I am serious about this promise, and you will recognize it from the prompt reply to your last two letters. And now another question. You write some of the war stories but forgot to notify me if our brother Jean had to go to the border, or stayed at home. I am very restless about it because his absence must be very distressing and difficult for you. Is he still in his old position? I have not received any news from Mr. Busch for 2½ years. He has left three of my letters unanswered, and since I heard that he had moved away from Haagen I have not written to him for two years. Since I have now learned from you where he is I will write to him later. Be so kind and greet Mrs. Lipp warmly for me and tell her that I would like to inquire about her son in Springfield. I certainly do not want to spare my own effort, but first of all, I have no address for him in Springfield, secondly there are at least 15 Springfields in the United States, the best known being in Illinois, another in Missouri, and so on, and third, all of these Springfields are almost as far away from Galveston as Basel is from Jerusalem. Those states are far to the north, and I live in the south. But I want to inquire about the address of a preacher in Springfield, Missouri as it is likely that Jean Lipp moved there from St. Louis, which is also close in Missouri, or to Springfield in Illinois, which the state of Missouri adjoins. That an unknown person demands money from Mrs. Lipp is obscene and most likely a fraud. If Jean really is not at home, you either have to keep the enclosed bill of exchange until he comes back or give it to him to endorse it to mother or to Mr. Siegrist. He will be accepted by any banker in Basel at full value.

Brother Wendt has paid off all of his debts here. He tells me that he has become the father of a third daughter. Tomorrow I will be standing with a child of Wendt's brother-in-law's brother-in-law, who is still living here. This is the seventh child I have baptized. One of my godchildren died, one is in the state of Pennsylvania, two in New Orleans, one in western Texas, 400 miles from here, two go to school with me, and were there before they were baptized. People often neglect baptism for too long. I saw one of my oldest students baptized with three of his siblings three years ago. On that day, Brother Wendt baptized 18 children together in the church. For now I want to close again putting everything I said to my heart. Always remember me in your intercession. Greet all the dear friends in Basel, Inzlingen and Haagen, especially our dear mother and brother Jean. Be commanded to the Lord by the heart of your brother Friedrich Gloor.

A BRIDE IS FOUND AND
A DISPUTE AT THE CHURCH

October 1, 1859 Galveston, Texas

Dear Sister!

This time I let you wait for an entire month for an answer. But that is more your fault than mine. I did not receive your last letter until the end of August because it had to be sent from Galveston to me in the interior of the country, where I was on vacation for all of August. Through a long round trip I was looking for relaxation from the strenuous work that becomes difficult here in summer. Only on the return trip did I find your letter in Brenham, which had been kept for me at the local post office. I would have gladly answered you right away but just the unfriendly, really loveless tone in which you write made me doubt whether I should answer at all and whether my answer would be pleasant for you. In my last letter I opened my heart to you and conveyed to you without any hesitation an important concern. I hoped to receive from you sisterly, friendly advice, a sympathetic, affectionate word; instead you write some indifferent lines about it and fill the rest of the letter with political news. I have always longed for your letters but this time my longing was deceived. But, I cannot blame you. I have not earned the love that you have already shown me, and it was a presumption of mine to want to demand more.

You wonder, dear sister, why I speak of marriage so early. I would like to give you two things to consider. First, I live in Texas, a country with a tropical, hot climate, where life develops quickly and dies away early. Secondly, since we saw each other last, about five years ago, I am not lucky enough to be with parents whose house I could regard as my home, but have been a stranger to strangers for so long. What that means, to be alone in a foreign land for five years, is that I must experience many temptations, and much struggle. Now, I am 24 years old, while in this climate married men of 19 and women of 15 years are very common. Also, I remember having already written to you earlier, that my position here absolutely requires that I create my own home. I do not want to annoy you if you cannot see how this is the case, but it is impossible for me to explain it to you more clearly. If you were here yourself, and all the circumstances became known to you, you would be surprised that I remained lonely for so long. Of all the brethren who arrived before me, with me, and two years after me, all are now married except Brother Moegle and Schumacher, who every day look forward to the arrival of their brides.

You also write that you would not say much (or maybe it should mean you did not care much about it) if I married a local girl unknown to you. These words have kept me from writing so far, and what I am writing now, I write mainly for the dear mother. She certainly will not be indifferent to the most important step in my life, and I will not do what I would like to do without her knowledge and blessing. A few days after the receipt of your letter in which you declared that you did not know anyone among your friends who were in accordance with my wishes, and you declared you were not quite satisfied with my intention, I got engaged to the daughter of a farmer in Texas. I got to know my present love bride 3 years ago, but it was not until my last trip to the countryside that I became acquainted with her through a meeting of various circumstances and incidents, and got to know her childlike faith, her loyalty, and change. When your letter came, I had so little hope of obtaining a life-companion from the old home, that I resolved, after earnest prayers and scrutiny from all those who spoke of it and against it, to speak with dear Brother Ebinger. His family belongs to the community in which I shall soon be received. Brother Ebinger could only approve of my intention, since he had known the individual for a long time and confirmed it himself. Two days before my departure from Galveston, I accompanied Brother Ebinger to the farm of my future father-in-law, which lies 70 miles from the coast, in the lonely forest. There I introduced my intention to the dear people, who have known me for a long time. The elderly parents gave me their gracious consent and blessing and the daughter gave me her yes. Her name is Therese Wuenscher. She was born in Germany, in Prussia, but came to Texas at an early age and is now 20 years old. Her father owns a large farm, which he works with his wife and two sons, one of whom will be confirmed this year. He plants mostly cotton. My dear bride will stay with her parents until the New Year, and then, perhaps will make the journey here in Brother Ebinger's company. Since she lives 200 miles from here, I will not see her again before the New Year. I hope and believe to have found a faithful and fitting wife when the Lord blesses our union, and thank the dear God who has directed my steps. What I still wish for is the blessing of our dear mother. I beg you, dear sister, since, in spite of your letter, I cannot believe that you really should be so indifferent to such a necessary and important step by your brother. Be so good, and share this with my dear mother and tell her that I ask you, urgently and childlike, to send me a word of love and blessing over our union before the appointed time. It would be very calming and provide inner peace for me, and I could then look forward to the future with joy and peace. Also, as soon as I know that you are pleased, I will ask my beloved bride to write to you, and being a pious, believing, virgin, and by faith in the Lord Jesus already related to you in the spirit. I hope that you both will soon love each other without seeing each other. Also, dear sister, write me your answer so that I can also send it to my Therese for reading. If you answer immediately after receiving this letter I can receive your answer in the beginning of December.

There has been a change in our church. There had been disputes between the congregation and Brother Ehinger in which neither side wanted to yield. I too could not get along with Brother Ehinger anymore than I could the first time, and had already stated my position to return to New Orleans, where I receive a call every month. The intolerable, domineering character of Brother Ehinger had forced me to leave the first time. My successor was only here three months and his successor was only here one day; then he fled from the yellow fever and did not return. I heard from him when I visited him on my last journey that he feared Brother Ehinger's intolerance. For the same reason, at the beginning of July, I needed to explain that I would have to leave the church again in three months. It was only the unanimous desire of the church that prompted me to withdraw my resignation, and to try to see if I could maintain with God's help, even under such oppressive circumstances. Soon, however, as a result of the exclusion of some parishioners by Brother Ehinger, new disputes broke out, which at last led the congregation and the preacher to come before the secular court. Here the dispute was decided in favor of the congregation, and during my absence Brother Ehinger was removed from the community. He left for the north this week and did not leave a good impression here because of the way he left. The church is now without a preacher, but has chosen Brother Ebinger, who may come in a few months. Until then the congregation has instructed me to conduct the services and has requested confirmation of this assignment from the Synod. These events have caused me much grief and sorrow, and in doing so, damage has been done to our congregation. The congregation can only be healed by the Lord sending us a faithful, sincere, and humble servant of His Word, a faithful Shepherd.

Well, dear sister, forgive me, if I do something wrong by this letter. I wait with longing for an answer, to clarify that to me, which is inexplicable to me in your last letter.

With warm regards to you, dear mother and Jean, your brother Fritz.

THE CIVIL WAR, BLOCKADE
AND THE BATTLE OF GALVESTON

There is a long lapse in letters from Friedrich to home between 1959 and 1964. The Civil War has caused it to be difficult, if not impossible, to get letters out. Galveston is surrounded by Northern warships, which create a blockade of its harbor. He gives a firsthand account of the Battle of Galveston on New Year's Day of 1863. On New Year's Eve, thousands of Confederate soldiers entered Galveston with cannons, and Friedrich and others fled to the protection of the sand dunes as cannonballs raced by them.

April 13, 1864 Galveston, Texas

Beloved mother and siblings!

For the first time, after such a long time, I sit down to give you, dear ones, a small sign of life in my beautiful, happy home. I sent a few lines to you two years ago. But I am afraid that the ship's captain, who wanted to take my note and me to Jamaica, was caught on the way. I did not see him again. Most likely, this letter will have the same fate, for 10 large warships now block our harbor; but still sometimes a nimble little schooner or steamer manages to get through the fog on a gloomy night. I do not want to apologize for my former long silence. If I live I hope to come to you in peace after the war,

Sketch made by George Grover of blockading Union ships at Galveston in 1864. *Courtesy of the Rosenberg Library.*

but for today I will write only the least, for I am in a great hurry since the complacent friend, who wants to take these lines with him, wants to take the first favorable opportunity to smuggle his boat through the blockade fleet. You have been in great anxiety about me since you know how terribly war rages on us. You may have already heard of how great fear and distress has come over our poor Galveston. Oh, how many times have I thought of you, dear ones, and your peaceful, blessed home during the hours of the most terrible danger here. But in all the distress and tribulation, the dear God has kept both me and my dear wife, who has faithfully remained at my side in every danger, intact.

The most terrible day we had to go through was New Year's Day of last year. A fleet of Northern warships lay in our harbor, which they had conquered three months earlier. They were close to the city, barely a stone's throw from the first houses; the next ship was only a few hundred paces from my apartment. On New Year's night 5,000 Confederate soldiers with canons etc., in complete silence, came across the nearly one hour long railway bridge, which connects the island with the mainland and about two hours before the city. We, the peaceful inhabitants of the city, hardly thought of danger; we thought we had already come through the worst of the war. Almost everyone was asleep when the army entered the city in deep silence. I didn't go to sleep until 2 a.m. At 4 a.m. I was awakened by a friend who had stayed awake and heard the cannons quietly crunching in the sand of

Sketch by George Grover of the Battle of Galveston Harbor during the Civil War. *Courtesy of the Rosenberg Library.*

the street. We got up quickly, awoke our neighbors, and then fled to the southernmost end of the city farther from the ships. In the house of a friend, whom we had to wake up from sleep, we found a friendly welcome. We thought we would stay here because we believed that the ships would only shoot cartridges, which did not fly that far, into the city. After a half hour of anxious waiting we heard the first cannon shot from the city thunder from the ships. The silence of the night suddenly made way for the most horrible crashes and roaring. The dense darkness of the night disappeared before the incessant flashes of cannons and small gunfire that was directed at the ships from the houses on the [*harbor*] beach. But now the ships responded and not only with cartridges, but also with bombs and all sorts of projectiles that swept through the entire city; some whizzing across the city and into the Gulf, so traveling over the whole width of the island. One of the first bombs shattered the neighboring house to the right where we were staying and another through two neighboring houses to the left. So we were not safe in our haven and we had to flee further. On our way to the sand dunes on the Gulf shore we often had to throw ourselves flat on the ground to avoid bullets or bombs dropping in front and behind us. A bomb flew so close to us that we felt the awful pressure of the air. The tinder of it was almost burned down; it could burst at any moment; it drove right in front of us through a sand dune in which the burning igniter was suffocated. We now sat down behind a protective sand dune, which had been used to serve as a battery, and wait for the day to dawn. The shooting continued incessantly. In the meantime the Northern ships had been attacked by some of the Southern steamers, and at the same time as we dared to climb to the top of the sand dune, the dreadful spectacle of a land and naval battle presented itself. One of the Southern gunboats was drilled into the ground at dawn while another managed to board and capture the best of the Northern ships [*the* Harriet Lane]. A short but terrible fight now ensued on the deck of the boarded ship. It was conquered, and this conquest decided the battle. It is true that the struggle on the part of the other ships continued for a while; but the shooting ceased, ending right at 8 o'clock. One of the Northern ships had landed on a sandbar and had been set afire by the Northerners themselves [*the* Westfield]. When the fire reached the powder chamber, it blew up with a terrible explosion. The commanding officer of the Northern fleet, who had carelessly spent too long a time aboard the burning ship with eight men, found his death. The rest of the ships left the harbor, but left behind in the hands of the victors the conquered Northern steamer along with two large sailing ships, that could not sail away and in the hurry of flight could not be set afire. But the battle had cost the blood of the victors too, and I still shudder at the memory of the spectacle that we experienced when we returned to the city. For a few days there was great disorder in the re-conquered city, and we lived in constant fear of our own victorious soldiers, five of whom, the day after the battle, invaded my quarters and demanded food. I spoke to them in a friendly manner, and we set before them what we had, cornbread and meat, and they became friendlier and moved on without stealing anything. Many other houses were plundered.

A few days later we were bombed from the Gulf by another Northern fleet, which has since been repeated from time to time; but we are still wonderfully spared, no bullet hit our house yet. Several times I have had to flee the school with the schoolchildren because bullets flew over them; but even my dear old schoolhouse has not suffered any damage except for a few windows that were broken by the shock. Thank God who has so graciously saved us so far!

In other respects too, I have to thank the Lord daily; I am one of the few men here who are free of military service. The law frees preachers and teachers of all military service who have taught at least twenty children since the beginning of the war. I have a very busy school at the moment, and I am also the only teacher in the city who has continued the school at all times; even while most of the inhabitants fled. However, I shouldn't count that much to my credit, since I was often close enough to lose my courage and leave the island city, which has been exposed to all kinds of danger, had my dear wife not remained so steadfast throughout all the horrors. I cannot describe to you at this time many details of the war to which we are now almost accustomed; the many bombardments and other dangers that we have endured and endure almost daily still. Only, in order to give you a concept of the prevailing situation, I must tell you the prices that we currently have to pay for groceries. One pound of flour costs 2½ dollars, or about 13 francs; a pound of coffee 24 dollars or 125 francs; a pair of boots 400 dollars, that is more than 2,000 francs; a pair of shoes 150 dollars; one pound of raw sugar 5 dollars or 25 francs; a sheet of stationary 1 dollar; a steel spring 1 dollar; etc. Everything is rationed. To be sure, my salary has been greatly increased; I also receive regular consignments of food from my parents-in-law, who live in the country; but you can imagine that, given the incredibly high prices of all the necessities of life, we must be grateful to God from the bottom of our hearts if we only have the most essential things, and we have never suffered from this until today. We planted a garden with vegetables; eggs are supplied to us by the chickens, which were stolen from us, but were replaced by gifts from others. As we have so often experienced the merciful help of the Lord, I hope that when the dear God revives life and healthy limbs, I will be able to report after the war.

Jean, my dear, dear brother, be so kind and send these lines to Mr. Prof. Bohnenberger in Blaubeuren, Wuerttemberg. His son, my dearest friend, is our preacher; he eats with us. He is healthy and lively, and with self-sacrificing loyalty, he has taken care of the poor and sick in this difficult time of suffering. His people will be glad to hear from him. He intends to write when another ship can break the blockade; maybe then at least one or the other letter will arrive over there. Oh, how I wish you would receive this letter that it still finds you alive and well. How hard it is now on my heart not to have written to you earlier before our connection was cut off. Daily I ask God to let me live the joy, to hear from you, dear mother and siblings again. How are you? Oh, that I would have wings to leave war and misery behind and be able to hurry to you for only one day. Farewell, dear ones, live well in God's protection. Keep your son and brother in a loving heart, Fried. Gloor

[Written above the head and at the left margin of the first page: *"My warmest greetings and kisses, dear brother, faithful, dearly beloved sister! Oh that I could tell everything, what moves my heart! But I have to stop as my heart is so full that I do not know where to start. God is with you; goodbye, good health.*

Greetings from my dear wife to all of you. Farewell, beloveds, and remember your far-off son and brother in loving prayer."]

THE BLOCKADE CONTINUES

Since letters are able to leave Galveston through the blockade with schooners that sneak past the enemy warships and travel to Mexico, his letters finally arrive in Basel. Yellow fever continues to plague Galveston, in addition to the war and its hardships.

December 7, 1864 Galveston, Texas

Dear mother and siblings!

I sent my last letter to you through a friend who wanted to try, with a small schooner at night, to secretly break through the enemy warships, which still block our harbor. Since then, I have heard that he has managed, after cross and transverse journeys, to enter a small port in Mexico, from where he left for the island of Cuba. I hope he sent my letter to the post office in Havana, and that you have it, albeit very late. I have told you in what tribulation we live here, what difficult times still lay ahead. Since then I have sent a letter to Professor Bohnenberger through a steamship leaving here. I reported to him the death of his son, our previous preacher. I asked him to write to you, since at that time I had no time to do this myself. The steamer has also happily come back and will try to sneak away again tonight. The friend to whom I gave the letter for Professor Bohnenberger told me that he had gotten it to the post office in the West Indies and offered to take another one back today. So I only have time to write a few lines. It is already night and in half an hour the ship wants to sail out. So, only the necessary words now. Since my last letter, our city has not yet been bombed again. But we still have to expect an attack every day. On the other hand, we have been terribly haunted by yellow fever this autumn. Over a few weeks, more than 300 people have died of it, although the city has barely half as many inhabitants as before. These inhabitants have all been here for years, since we have had no immigration here for four years. I could not hold school for three months. In August I made a horseback trip around the country, riding about 300 miles from one settlement to another; visiting many friends and acquaintances. Strengthened in heart and soul, I returned at the beginning of September and received the sad news that my dear friend, our preacher Bohnenberger, unexpectedly, quickly died during my absence. As there is no possibility for our congregation to receive another preacher immediately, I was willing to abide by a decision of the congregation, and by the request of the Synod to accept the office of preacher. I will remain as preacher as long as I feel that this is not my profession, but just until we can get another preacher. Galveston, because of its location on the seacoast, is the place most exposed to the dangers of war; therefore, I believe that during the war no preacher will be agreeable to come here. In September and October, I was ill and watched by a nurse day and night, and I experienced terrible episodes. Often the black vomiting of yellow fever sufferers is sprayed over my face and hands. Many patients are restless and they must be watched closely. I often went to funerals to the field of God [*cemeteries*] with a funeral procession and then, as others followed suit, had to go from one grave to another to deliver the funeral orations. My wife too got the terrible disease, but the dear God blessed her with quickly applied help, so that after only three days she was out of danger, and a week later she was able to do her household work again. Despite all the work and constant vigils, getting only two nights of sleep in the worst week, the Lord has kept me healthy. This is the first fall since I arrived in Texas where I have gotten through it without illness. The plague has now ended, but many families are in mourning. Among the many friends whom the terrible plague has taken away is Frau Maser from Wuerttenburg, with whom I used to eat dinner, and of whom I wrote to you in my earlier letters. In spite of the unbelievably high prices of food I have never suffered, and I have been paid 150 dollars in gold by the government this autumn in recognition of my having taught the children of soldiers and orphans for free. Most of the money now in circulation is paper money. Gold and silver are very rare and are disappearing more and more. The prices in paper money are still rising, so now a pair of boots is 1000 dollars, a pound of coffee 35 dollars, a pound of flour 6 dollars, a pound of meat 3 dollars, a pound of butter 25 dollars and so on. A sheet of paper costs 2 dollars. For emergencies I now have a small sum in gold and silver. If it were possible, I would like to send you something but it is too unsafe and would be lost if the ship were caught. I would be happy to finally hear something from you again. D. Weber from Basel now has a school here too. During the yellow fever he stayed on the island with his father-in-law. He has been married for some time. If you wish to write to me, address the letter: Mr. F. Gloor, care of Mr. Jul. Frederich / Houston, Texas, / and place it in a second envelope that you address to Messrs. Droege, Oetling&Co. / Matamaras, Mexico / the letter must be posted, so that I am sure to get it. You cannot believe with what melancholy I always think of you, how much I wish to hear from you once again, my dears. I have to close. Many sincere greetings to all friends and acquaintances, especially to Stocklin's, Karl Roth and Pastor Respinger, Mr. Gysin and all. The Lord be with you and greetings to you and yours / Friedrich Gloor.

December 17, 1864 Galveston, Texas

Dear mother and siblings!

Although I sent you a letter a few days ago through a blockade runner, I do not want to abandon a safe opportunity to write to you again in the hope that of the many letters I have sent lately, at least one comes into your hands. The commanding general here to all civilians, has allowed all to leave the city next Monday. All who wish to use this permission will be taken under a white truce flag to the enemy warships in front of our harbor, from where they will be sent to New Orleans. Since New Orleans has long been in the hands of the Northerners, that is, no longer blocked. I want to give these lines to a family I know will give them to the post office. May this letter come to your hands soon, and meet you as healthy and well as it leaves me!

Of course I cannot make use of the given permission to leave. I hardly think that it applies to me. For although I'm not yet a soldier, I would be subject to military service the moment I resigned because only my job has freed me from military service so far. Now that the preacher is dead and I

Sketch of the Civil War and military affairs during the Civil War in Galveston and the capture of *Harriet Lane*, as depicted by George Grover. *Courtesy of the Rosenberg Library.*

am alone in the church and have to administer the office of preacher and teacher, I could not live with my conscience if I left my post. Come what may, I will stay here as long as a person can stay here. So far dear God has helped me through some terrible dangers; in his hand we are also under the horrors of war; I also want to trust in his help. Therefore, since my wife is of the same mind, I have so far refused several very advantageous positions that were offered to me in the country. We decided so even though it is now much easier and safer to live in the country than here, where we face the danger of an attack every day, exposed to enemy gunboats. If you have received the letter I sent you last summer, you will have read what dangers we faced two years ago, how the enemy cannonballs, bombs, and cartridges whizzed in all directions through our city.

It is very likely that the same attacks will begin again in the near future. It's mainly for this reason that I write to you so often because I don't know how long I will have the opportunity. You shouldn't resent me for not writing in the first years of the war; at that time there was not as much opportunity as there is now. A few months ago the blockade has become less common, as it was a year ago when we were quite cut off from the rest of the world, since the route through Mexico was also very unsafe. What worries me a lot is the fact that I have not heard from you for several years except through a letter from Pastor Ebinger, who wrote more than two years ago, and reported that he visited you, and that you are all still alive. Often I fear that over this long

Sketch of the destruction of the *Westfield* by George Grover. *Courtesy of the Rosenberg Library.*

period of time one or the other of you may have died; and I am anxiously waiting to receive news from you, dear ones. It has been nearly ten years since I saw you for the last time; I always hoped to be able to visit you again after ten years of separation; but this terrible war pushed the prospect of that joy far beyond. But my intention, if it pleases God to save my life, is to make a visit to my dear home some years after the end of the war. Oh, how happy I would be to see you again, with what sadness I always think of you, of my friends, of every little place in the old, lovely city of Basel. It is my life's deepest wish to be able to once more touch your heart, and once again to wander the old familiar streets of my beloved hometown. How beautiful and lovely your home is can only be appreciated when you have not seen it for a long time. How much may have changed in the long years! I was 19 years old; now I am in the 30th. The dear mother may well have aged very much in this time, especially since the blessed father is no longer there. Oh, that I, beloved mother, could once more touch your heart and tell you all that my heart is full of, and what I cannot put on paper! And my dear sister! How would I rejoice to look into your eyes again and bless you for the love and faithfulness with which you bore me in the most terrible time in my life! And yet I am glad that you didn't come here upon my earlier request, for what suffering and horror, what fear and need you would have found yourself in.

As much as I would like to have you with me, I thank the dear God that you decided not to leave the mother. But if this war is over and you ever lack a support, rest assured that if I am still alive my arms will always be open to you. What is my brother Jean doing? As bad as I sometimes angered him I always hope that he sometimes thinks of me kindly as Issac [*sic*] thought of his distant brother Jacob. Are you still with the haulage company or in the customs office? I long to hear how it is with you dear brother, how it is with all of you? Write very soon and give me a report about you and all friends. I would like to tell you once more how a letter from you can get into my hand in the safest way.

...

The paper and time have run out, I must close. May the Lord grant you a blessed Christmas and a happy New Year! Greet all friends from me; especially Pastor Respinger, Stocklins, Karl Roth (where is he?) and all those who ask for me. Farewell dear ones, maybe I'll write again soon! Greetings from yours / son and brother Friedrich Gloor.

PEACE REACHES THE EAST
BUT NOT YET GALVESTON

Smuggling is a way for Galveston to obtain provisions and send communications. Friedrich writes of men deserting their families to avoid enlistment in the Confederate army. The war east of the Mississippi River is over, but it is still very much a part of life in Galveston and parts of the South. Confederate soldiers loot and steal from the citizens of Galveston.

May 10, 1865 Galveston, Texas

Beloved mother and siblings!

To my unspeakable delight I received your letter from February 5th—four days ago. It had been on the road for 3 months. Never in my life has a letter given me such joy. It came in like a bright sunbeam into the dark night. My heart had been troubled on the very day that the dear letter was brought to me. Our political turmoil is now nearing its decision, and just the day your letter arrived news and orders came which promised an early end to the war, but also the prospect of the complete destruction of our poor city of Galveston. In my own home I had misery and distress before me, not concerning myself, but close enough to make my heart quite heavy. About six weeks ago 5 German women came down from the country with their children. Their husbands had earlier deserted the Southern army and now live in northern cities. Women of deserters have from time to time been sent under the white flag to the blockade ships where they have always been accepted to be transported to New Orleans by the regular fleet of mail vessels. The women wanted to use this travel opportunity; they had therefore sold all of their belongings in the country and unexpectedly arrived here, accompanied by the preacher Woerner of Spring Creek, whom Henriette still knows from Inzlingen. I took them all into my house and Brother Woerner returned to his house a few days later, leaving the women with me. I took the necessary steps for the poor people, acquired the necessary passports for them from the commanding general, and a few weeks later when the white flag was put on the blockade ships I took them out on the parliamentary boat to the fleet. That was about 14 days ago. Halfway there the wind died, we lay at anchor for several hours and had to use the tide to return to the harbor. The following morning we left with a favorable wind and after two hours arrived at the fleet, which on that day counted fifteen large, magnificent warships. We were told that the mail boat was no longer able to wait, and that they were not allowed to take women and children aboard their gunboats. So we had to leave without doing anything, and when 10 days later it was parliamentary, the officers of the fleet had received orders not to accept any more passengers from Galveston. As from the 1st of May strict quarantines were to be held in New Orleans because of the yellow fever. Now the good people are still in my house, one of the women and one child have already been seriously ill and of course they are greatly concerned about what to do now. According to the latest news, the war in the part of the country east of the Mississippi has already ended, and it is now hoped that peace will return soon; but I am afraid from some things that I notice here and there that there is still a desperate attempt to continue the resistance here in Texas. God grant that it does not come to that. Boundless misery would be the sure consequence of it.

So I was quite downcast last Saturday; the fate of the poor women worried me; I was at a loss for what to advise them, other concerns about the community, about the school, and about the future of our city. That was when Mr. Consul Fredrich, who had just arrived here from Houston, brought me the letter that had come to him from Mexico by post. Already at the address, I recognized where it came from, dear, good, Jean. I still recognize his handwriting after ten years: as small as mine. I could not wait until I came home with the letter; I had met Mr. Fredrich at the Houston Railroad. I ran into the first known house and opened the letter with my hands trembling with joy. Of course, the picture of my dear mother fell into my hands first. But it took a long time before I recognized the dear, dear, outlines of the good mother. In my mind I had always imagined her as I had left her; but I find in the lovely picture that the 10-½ years have not passed without clear traces about them. This change in the outlines caused by the years is probably more striking to me than you, since for me it is a sudden change, but for you is a gradual and unnoticed change that comes under your eyes. But as I was able to look at the picture with calmness, it was easy for me to find my dear, unforgettable mother in it. Oh, dear, good mother, you cannot know what great joy you have made! The Lord God bless you abundantly for the love that has saved your lost son thus far, and after such a long separation!

My wife was very happy about it. All my despondency was gone, I know now that you are still alive and still thinking of me. Since then I've had a real homesickness, and when God gives us that sweet peace again and I'm still alive I hope to surprise you with an unexpected visit. The desire to see you again, dear ones, in this time of war, during which I did not hear from you for so long, has become an irresistible yearning in me.

A few months ago I received a letter from Mr. Prof. Bohnenberger. I answered it in a moment but have not found an opportunity to send it, so my letter to him will probably be sent with this letter, and arrive at Mr. Prof. Bohnenberger's estate at the same time as you read these lines. The so-called blockade running, which has been great between here and Havana in the last ten months, has now almost completely stopped. The price of cotton has fallen very much and the unusually strong blockade fleet, which has been lying in front of our harbor for some time, is causing the risk of disruption of profit even more than it was before. Moreover, in the near future there is either peace or a serious attack on our city; but in either case, the smuggling ships would be lost. Although some money has come into the city due to the smuggling business, I do not mind seeing it stop. It is not only that the cessation of the blockade is a sure sign of the near peace, but it also stops one of the causes of the great lack of morality in our city. The men employed on the smuggling ships were for the most part the expulsion of humanity, and their influence was all too easy to recognize, especially among the younger female part of our population. In addition, the city has come into great danger at various times by the blockade running. Of course, the ships can only enter and leave on dark nights, as they have to sneak close to the northern gunboats. If the night is too dark and foggy, or the pilot too inexperienced, or, as it has already occurred, drunk, it is easily for such a ship, in an effort to keep as far away from the enemy as possible, to come too close to the land and gets stuck on the beach. This happened several times in a week; three times just in front of the south side of the city. [*The harbor is on the north side.*] When the day dawned the stuck ships were, of course, discovered by the local authorities and the fire immediately opened. Some people have been shot that way. Others, helped by the tide, were able to get away with the loss of part of the cargo. And, although always pursued with bullets and often shot through and through, still the smuggling ships managed to reach the safe harbor that is currently defended by strong batteries at its entrance. The city was always in some danger but this always passed mercifully, and although the city is largely in ruins, it seems very wonderful to me that it has not suffered further, and that it will be able to go through the various bombardments without being turned entirely into a pile of rubble and ash. The greatest damage our city has suffered so far is not attributable to the enemy cannonballs, but to our own soldiers. You could not imagine how they live. However, they were almost forced to do so because they received no money, no adequate clothing, no proper food, and not even the necessary firewood.

The 11th of May, 1865 Galveston, Texas

This evening came the news that the requested surrender of our state had been roughly refused and that after the fall of all the other states our poor Texas should continue the war on its own. If that happens, may the Lord be merciful to us! Yesterday, when I started this letter, we had such lovely hopes for peace that I thought I would be able to send it directly from here by post. This hope is now gone; the blockade has also stopped. In Mexico the civil war rages like ours. Matamoras is besieged by the liberals, so for the time being no letter can be sent through this place. So, now I have as little chance of sending you my response as I did two or three years ago. But I want to go on writing day by day, and wait patiently, until there is another chance somewhere. Some time ago I received a letter from my friend Ebinger in Zurich, also about Mexico. It worried me very much that he did not mention yours except that my letter to you from April last year had been sent to him, as well as the message of Pastor Bohnenberger's death. He did not write whether all of you are still healthy and alive, and that caused me much unrest. Finally, after so much waiting and hoping, I received the dear letter with the picture. I have Pastor Ebinger's letter that has not yet been answered but I will do so if I still have time at the next opportunity. In the meantime, I ask dear Jean to write to him, telling him that we still have no preacher, and probably will not receive one before the war ends. As you can easily imagine, my time is taken up so much that I only have the late evening to write letters, whereby I often cannot cope with the correspondence that I must maintain. Hence, it is that this letter, like the one that was sent to Prof. Bohnenberger a few days ago, is only being created piece by piece. For that reason you should not be surprised that I am writing without following a proper train of thought, just as it is with my heart, as if I was speaking to you verbally when you are with me.

MURDER IN THE STREETS

Friedrich describes the murder of a young Black girl and the subsequent shootout between her killer and a witness in front of the post office.

The 12th of May, 1865 12:30 a.m. Galveston, Texas

I cannot lie down to rest before talking to you a little bit. I just came home from a visit a short distance away, and am too excited to sleep. I must also smoke a pipe to keep the impertinent mosquitoes in check. This afternoon I witnessed a murder which throws a brighter light on the conditions here than a long essay, but which is also strange evidence that God's justice can reach where the arm of human justice cannot or will not suffice. A military doctor, Dr. McElmarry, a few month ago in conjunction with another officer, had seduced a young Negro girl to steal and bring the sum of $3,000 from the bedroom of her owner by promising to give her half the money and take her out to the blockade fleet from where she would then travel to New York and freely spend the money. The poor girl did the deed too, but instead of being taken to the blockade fleet, she was escorted out of town that night, deprived of her stolen money, and shot in the head by McElmarry. The case became apparent, suspicion fell on the two officers, and the evidence was so clear that it was believed that the two would be found guilty. On the pretext that there was too much prejudice against them, they were taken to Houston, and were acquitted, probably as a result of the generous use of the stolen money. Today, Dr. McElmarry came down from Houston with the outspoken intention of murdering a young man, named Sutton, who had witnessed against him. I was at the post office when they met in front of the post office building. McElmarry drew his pistol. Sutton, however, arrived before him and shot him through the abdomen, so that he died in horrible pain after half an hour. This happened in the bright day, at 4 p.m., in front of about 60 persons, who waited for letters because a post had arrived! Sutton was arrested and freed an hour later, having taken the life of his assailant in self-defense.

RECONSTRUCTION AND CITIZENS TAKE UP ARMS

The 18th of May, 1865 in the evening Galveston, Texas

I could not continue writing for a few days as I was very busy, and in my house, as in the city at the moment, almost everyone is sick. The whole traveling party, which is still with us, suffers from climatic diseases; a child has died of it today; another woman has become seriously ill, and of the five women, three are sick and the other two feel unwell. My wife too, has not been quite well for some time. I was chilled 14 days ago and still cough a bit, but I am the healthiest one in the house and the only one who has an appetite for food. Almost no house in the city is spared from illness but, not uncommonly, many people die. The diseases are probably due to the dreadful downpours we have had throughout the winter and now suddenly followed by the most pressing heat, that is not much relieved even at night! Our Texas, taken as a whole, has a very bad climate; too dry or too wet, too hot or too cold. Yesterday a man stabbed another in the street in a quarrel over a log of wood that everyone said was owned by him. Such conditions lead to the Civil War!

Postwar lawlessness leaves Galveston citizens to take up arms to protect themselves.

The 22nd of May, 1865 Galveston, Texas

God, the Lord, thank you! The gravest concerns are over; we have a clear chance for peace soon. The last three days have been a troubled time for us. The most contradictory rumors were in circulation; the generals sought to encourage the soldiers to fight for life or death in every possible way. But the soldiers themselves are tired of the war. Everywhere they began to speak out. Today was the deciding factor; it was an eventful day for us. Last night came an order that the army be dissolved and should evacuate the island within two days. At daybreak one of the Southern government's smugglers arrived in the harbor with a full load of clothes, saddles, leather goods, and so on. The troops, who had not received any payment for 18 months, fell on the ship and plundered it outright. It had a value of several hundred thousand dollars. The officers of courage left and all the troops were dissolved. Many of them were sent into the country by train and steamboat, and the powder magazines at the various forts were blown up. In addition, a parliamentary flag came in from the blockade fleet and demanded the surrender of the city, which will probably not be refused. So we are now confident that the bloodshed, the constant fear and danger in which we have been living for four years, must finally give way to at least a tolerable state. But we still have serious concerns. Many of this morning's plunderers are still here, and seem to have been encouraged by the successful attack on the ship to do similar things in houses. Few citizens will go to bed tonight, as people are generally afraid that attempts will be made to set the city on fire to plunder. I also intend to watch at least part of the night. Our mayor summoned the entire citizenry this evening through sounding the alarm bells in the market house, and asked us to stand firm together to prevent acts of violence being perpetrated on individuals by lawless and disorderly soldiers. After tonight all citizens will be provided with weapons and ammunition. This lawless state will last until the Northern fleet takes possession of the city. May the Lord allow that this will happen soon, and we will be redeemed from this pitiful state! I think a lot these days about my unforgettable friend Bohnenberger. How much would he now rejoice in the prospect of the end of the war, as he longed for peace! Yes, well him! He has found a better, and the only true, eternal peace! I hope to be able to send you this letter by regular mail, and I look forward to receiving your reply quickly, and regularly. You, too, will surely rejoice with us and thank the Lord, who has saved us in so many misfortunes and perils; and even averted all shortcomings in the common emergency. Before you receive this letter, you will probably have news of the end of the war and will be able to think of me with less concern than before. The first post that leaves here is to take this letter, and I will count the days until I have another answer from you.—It is 12:30 a.m. The alarm bell is ringing again to summon citizens to receive weapons. I will not go, I do not want to put my trust in gunpowder, but rather in the Gentleman who will continue to protect the city. I want to command His mighty protection, and I want to rest for the night, while you have probably gotten up now because it is already after 6 a.m. for you. Good night, beloveds, all, the Lord, our God, be our protection and umbrella!

The 27th of May, 1865 in the evening Galveston, Texas

The last five days were an exciting time for us again. The reaction happened quickly and with terrible violence. The same people that could be furious two months ago when there was talk of capitulation are now unanimously demanding peace at all costs. Attitudes that would have brought you to the gallows a quarter of a year ago are now pronouncements heard openly and loudly. The same people who three weeks ago swore eternal hatred and mortal combat to the North cannot wait until the Northerners will take possession of the state with their fleets and armies. What a fickle creature man is, especially here in America!

This tremendous reaction did not, however, take place without encountering resistance here and there. As I told you five days ago, after the local troops had plundered a blockade-runner; they moved to our neighboring city of Houston, where they joined forces with the regiments stationed there. Still excited by the plundering which had taken place in Galveston, the militia now chased the officers away, threw themselves on the buildings containing government supplies, and endeavored to destroy everything that they could not carry away. The citizens of Houston trembled in anticipation of general looting but the soldiers generally respected all private property and contented themselves with the public supplies. When there was nothing left to steal the wild bands scattered and everyone headed home with weapons and luggage without saying goodbye. But there were still individuals who do not have a permanent home, mostly neglected, dangerous people. General Magruder then made the desperate plan to gather another 1,500–2,000 men among these post-sailors and vagabonds, to lead them back to Galveston to continue the desperate struggle here as much as possible. General Magruder is the same one who reconquered our city New Year's Day 1863 along with a few ships. If Texas now submits to the Northern government, he must leave the country and seek salvation in a swift flight. He knows the fate that threatens him, and that makes him angry and unforgiving. His last defensive plan failed because of the firmness of our city authorities, which declared that it would be better to destroy the railroad than to allow the return of the worst part of the army back into the city. However, General Magruder found the most resistance among the soldiers themselves, of whom only fifteen volunteered instead of two thousand, but the rest, when the general wished to hold one of his accustomed boastful speeches, cried out to him: "Shut your mouth, you cotton-thief!" And that's the same man who was almost idolized just a few weeks ago. Innocent citizens could have been thrown into jail without anyone daring to speak out against such injustices. What an unexpected change! A few days ago the governor of Texas sent two envoys to New Orleans to meet with the Northern general to establish the conditions under which the state should return to the Union. The decision will be determined in a few days. It may be what it sounds like; that peace is now certain to us. For us, the prospect is at least ten more months of taxation and lack of income; but the Lord, who has so lovingly preserved us so far, in so much distress and danger, will also help us through the troubles still to come!

The 29th of May, 1865; afternoon.

I noticed only now that this letter is getting the look of a diary. The only cause of this persistent listing is the uncertainty regarding the conveyance of the letter. If, as I had a few months before, I had the opportunity to send letters through Havana, the first part of this letter would have been on its way a long time ago. So the letter always remains open on my desk, and as I have time or am in the right mood, I sit down and patch another rag onto it. This will be a piece so long that you should be happy if you get through the reading in one evening. By the way, if you see my small handwriting for this evening, brother Jean will have to read it to you for he seems to have excellent eyes. At least he wrote me a little note, barely as big as a Basel treat (Oh, if I had one!), which, if it had been written in ordinary handwriting, would have made a very respectable letter. Six of his words extend an inch. Luckily, God has at least blessed me with one sharp eye, the left one—my right eye is significantly short-sighted; otherwise I would have had to use my microscope to help. The steamer that has so far carried my letters to you and to Professor Bohnenberger to Havana to the post office is called 'Donvigh'. She has been here more often and has had better luck in its dangerous travels than any other blockade-runner. But a few days ago she came to a terrible end. I have told you above of the day the soldiers tore up the bonds of discipline. A steamer loaded with government supplies entered the harbor and was looted. The crew of this ship said that the 'Donvigh' was still on its way, since they had, of course, not yet learned in Havana anything about our local conditions. Of course, it was foreseen that she would have a similar fate as her predecessor. But it got worse. As everything in our city was upside down, the lamp in the local lighthouse was no longer lit. I think it was stolen or broken. The 'Donvigh' arrived at the harbor in the dark of night, passed happily through the blockade fleet; but as the guiding light was out, she could not find the entrance channel and ran aground. Immediately after daybreak the blockade ships discovered the stranded vessel and opened a terrible cannonade on it. Soon after, we saw much smoke rising from the ship, and it was not long before the whole beautiful ship was engulfed in flames. The crew rescued themselves in small boats to shore but all the rich cargo became a victim of the flames.

Since the time you received the letters from the previous year, I have sent two more letters via New Orleans, one to Mr. Gysin, the other to you. Both will, as I hope, have arrived properly, but surely Mr. Gysin will have received his earlier than you, although the former was written later. If I am not mistaken, I wrote the letter to you in November or December and gave it to a woman who hoped to travel through the blockade fleet under the white flag to New Orleans, where her husband had deserted. I wrote to Mr. Gysin in January and gave the letter to another woman who was going on the same journey. The latter managed to reach her goal sooner, and so unexpectedly fast that I did not have time to fetch the letter from the other woman, who was also promoted soon afterwards. May the Lord grant that all these letters, as well as the present ones, may find you all healthy!

The 13th of June 1865 Galveston, Texas

The last 14 days have been such a busy time for me that I have never been able to write by daylight and writing in candle light which attacks my eyes so much that I try again today for the first time. Peace is now finalized.

Praise to the Lord and thank you for that! The Northern warships have been peacefully in port for eight days, and the officers are walking around the city unhindered. But we do not have a postal connection with foreign countries yet; but it will not be long before the former traffic is allowed to be restored.

The day before yesterday I was greatly pleased. I received a letter from dear Mr. Gysin von Inzlingen. I do not have time yet to answer it before the end of this letter, so please ask sister Henriette to tell him that I received his letter and to thank him cordially in my name. The loving writing is not only very interesting to me because of its rich content, but it particularly pleases me through the fatherly love, which radiates out of every line of it. Once the regular postal service has been restored, I will not fail to answer it, and especially to reply to the church news from Baden with church news from Texas.

In my previous letters I have never mentioned anything about my friend Daniel Weber. I call him my friend because he has become one. I never wrote about him because I could not write good things and I didn't want to share my suspicions with anyone else. But now he has made such a radical change that I can gladly give news of him. He spent his first years in Texas with adventurous roaming. First he was a teacher for Pastor Braun in Houston; then he came here and worked a few weeks for a magazine. From there he went back into the country and was a waiter at a restaurant in Hempstead for some time. Then he had a small shop in Bastrop where he poured beer. Then he wanted to go to Mexico but only got as far as San Antonio. In the fall of 1860 he came back here, poor and abandoned. I then helped him set up a small school on the island a few miles from here, but his unsteady nature soon drove him away again. Ebinger, Bohnenberger, and myself assisted him with a travel allowance to go to Brazoria on the Brazos River, where he opened a school but had to give it up in 1862 in the wake of the war. From there he came back without my knowledge and stayed longer on the island about six miles away, hiding with his present father-in-law because he was afraid of having to become a soldier, since he had no school anymore. There he was also safe during the terrible bombing of the New Year in 1863. A few days after the New Year, when the city was again in Confederate hands, he ventured into the city to open a school, but he had barely entered the city and was taken to a harbor fortress, that lies on a small sandbank in the middle of the water, without being allowed to see me, or let me know. He firmly refused to take the oath but had to practice daily with guns, watchmen duties and so on.

After eight days he received 24 hours of leave to get his clothes. On this occasion I saw him again for the first time. In a hurry he opened a private school, and after many efforts with the general and other officers, and after visiting all the offices, he finally got his papers. The matter was so difficult because the law only acquitted the teachers who had been teachers two years before the war and had remained uninterrupted, and because he had no school at the time when he was conscripted. His school is now in a very prosperous state; he married and lives hardly a few hundred paces from me. We visit almost daily if time permits and last Sunday I baptized his little son of whom I am the godfather also. His whole being is changed; he is a very good man worthy of consideration and has become a very dear friend to me that I testify to him with all the more great joy since I was very suspicious of him for a long time. He promised me that he would write to his mother and to Mr. Gysin in the near future. A steamboat arrived today from New Orleans with paroled prisoners of war that will leave tomorrow. Hoping to find an opportunity to send this letter; I hereby want to close it. But, first a few words to the dear brother Jean.

So, you've become a homeowner, dear brother, and a big man, boss of billing control, or whatever that means, as well as husband and father. That was very surprising and good news for me, but especially the latter. I have not gotten so far as to own my own house, and we are still childless, although once in the third year of our marriage we had hope of experiencing the joys of being parents. Even now we have not given up this hope and it would be a great joy for us if the Lord would answer our prayer for posterity. I sincerely wish you, dear brother, good luck and God's abundant blessing to your house, your office and your family. How happy would I be to be able to get to know your wife and my little niece, whom I love without knowing her because she is yours. Should such happiness ever be granted to me? I almost doubt it, and yet I like to think so much about the possibility. But for the time being I have to be patient. If it should be that I may once make a visit to the dear home, God will show me ways and means. Dear brother, I have a request of you. If some of the Chrischona brothers are looking to come to Texas in the coming autumn, I would like to ask you to send with the Brothers a number of Basel newspapers, Volksbote, newly published books that you think will be of interest to me, etc., even if they are old. We have been so cut off from the world that it is hard to keep up with everything. I particularly would like the Volksboten for the years 1864 and 65. Also, be so good and ask if the letters from me for the two years are still available—the one in 1855 and the other, from the summer of 1857, in which the fire of the steamer 'Louisiana' is described. I'd like to see them and refresh old memories with them. Let the delivery company pay you the costs for which I want to reimburse the expenses here.

I am very happy that my dear mother can live with you and I thank you, dear Jean, for everything you do to make her age easy and pleasant. May the Lord bless you for that. As soon as I can buy a secure exchange to a Swiss trading house, I would like to send you something again. The money is ready. Its purpose was to serve as an emergency penny in extreme need, or, if the dear God averted the extreme need, to be sent to the dear mother.

My wife thanks you for the greetings she has received and returns them most warmly. I would like to send the enclosed excerpt from a newspaper page to Mr. Prof. Bohnenberger. It contains his son's obituary as it appeared in the local newspaper. I forgot to include it in the letter to Prof. Bohnenberger. I have to close now. If the letter does not leave tomorrow I'll probably have time to fill in the rest of the space. My warmest regards to Pastor Roth. I would like to write to him, my unforgettable childhood friend, if I knew that he would be comfortable with it. I wrote to him in 1859 but never sent the letter; it is lying in front of me now and I am almost tempted to enclose the unfinished letter as it is here. But I would rather leave it alone and finish the letter buried so long in my portfolio and send it later. That my dear friend still loves me and shares in my fate, I am very happy. I thank him warmly for the love he has kept for me at all times, and also when I have made myself unworthy of it. May the Lord bless him for that. I will always remember him and the years of adolescence that I spent in his community [*church*]. I have always carefully kept his letters, which I received from him in earlier times in Basel and in Beuggen, and often reread them, and I still possess a tobacco pipe with his portrait, which I treasure highly.

That Theophil Stoecklin and his sister Tabitta have died causes me great sadness. Theophil was very dear to me; we grew up together. May the good God fill the hearts of the grieving parents with his living consolation! I greet them warmly, as well as Mr. Meister and his family at the Land Orphanage. I remember Ms. Speuermann quite well, and have not forgotten how good she was to me. That she has been ill for so long touches me deeply. May the Lord stand by her in grace and let this heavy visitation lead her to eternal salvation! May He give her patience in her grave sufferings and the sacred hope of the children of God!

The greeting from Mr. and Mrs. Maeglin is most heartily returned. Be all of you too, beloved ones, mother, brother, sister, brother-in-law, and your dear Louischen a thousand times greeted and kissed and commanded by the protection of our Lord and God / by yours faithfully in love of you / Friedrich Gloor. / NB. The promised picture of Brother Jean and my dear sister-in-law and the little dear Louischen is eagerly awaited. I cannot send ours until peace brings us a photographer. Art of this kind has been terribly neglected.

THE LAST KNOWN LETTER

April 18, 1866 Galveston, Texas

Dearly beloved mother and siblings!

I have hesitated replying for a long time now, beloved ones, to answer your dear letter of December last year and I have thought with sorrow and distress many times since then that you might therefore be alarmed or even cry out to me. Well, I don't like using the usual excuse to apologize for slipping, namely, 'I have not had the time'; for this time alone I have to ask you to accept this apology from me. I have been so busy over the past four months as never before in my life, and during that time I have only had time for the most necessary correspondence related to office and work. At the beginning of December I had to start confirmation lessons with 36 children. I had neglected to do so in the preceding year, partly because at that time we always still hoped to receive a preacher. I could not go beyond the essentials in regard to ecclesiastical functions, although I am licensed from the Synod to perform all ecclesiastical acts. That is partly because, at that time, the war had scattered our members far and wide. That has changed now. The congregation has regrouped, and it became necessary to celebrate the confirmation this year. So I have school daily from 8 a.m. to 2 p.m., hold confirmation classes from 3 p.m. to 5 p.m. and then a private lesson, often two, that keep me in the city. I had started these private lessons earlier, and was not now allowed to give up since it pays very well, and a quite welcomed addition to my income. The evening I had to use the time for the most necessary visits, and I used the late evening or early morning hours to prepare for the day's work. So it happened that I had to postpone writing to you from one time to another for so long, and I hope you will excuse me now in love because of my long silence. In spite of all this work I have, thank God, always remained very healthy and rested; my wife as well enjoys quite good health. Only last fall I was bedridden for eight days. I had a tooth removed, the first since being in America. The next day, a Saturday, I was called far out into the island about eight miles to marry a couple. It was a very warm day and I was picked up in an open carriage. Suddenly, while on the road, the sky clouded over and here came a fast emerging northern storm with rain. Since the following day was Sunday, I had to return to the city at night, where twice we slid off into the marshes in the dark and had to jump into the water to clear the carriage. The cold I contracted brought with it a violent fever and extremely painful inflammation of the tooth wound that tied me to the bed for a whole week. Since then I have not had any complaints or the slightest malaise.

Photograph of Galveston's customshouse, the first nonmilitary federal building erected in the state of Texas, completed in 1861. It served as a port of entry into the country, where government officials regulated commerce and collected shipping taxes. *Courtesy of the Rosenberg Library.*

There was a lot of work over the holidays. It was a very blessed day for me. On Palm Sunday, the confirmation took place. The first and probably last time I will do this action. The church was overcrowded, so that chairs and benches had to be brought in from neighboring houses and placed around the church. God grant that the celebration may be blessed for all present, especially for the confirmands themselves. It was a hard day for me, and never before have I felt more profound than in those hours. But God knows, I have never sought this ministry, and am glad to lay it down as soon as the newly awaited preacher arrives here. I was free to keep the preaching position in the local community; the church itself desired it; only my conscience forbids me. I do not feel called to do so and only the necessity and the supposition that it is God's will, not mine. After my dear friend Bohnenberger's death, this gives me the inner freedom to administer his office until a successor is found. By Brother Ebinger's efforts, as he writes to me, such a person has now been found, and I hope he has already begun his journey. The Lord guide him happily across the sea and place him among us as a rich blessing. I am looking forward to his arrival, and I believe, after all, what Brother Ebinger writes about him, that we will be here together in brotherly friendship. Our city has risen very quickly since the war ended. The shattered houses are quickly patched or rebuilt and trade has taken such an impressive boost that we now have a much larger population than at any time before the war. Nobody would have guessed that a year ago. But something that I believed in quite confidently has not arrived. I expected that through the plight and sorrow of war an effective and beneficial fruit for life in general would be obtained. There are few traces of this. On the contrary, godlessness of all kinds rises to the same extent that need diminishes and previous prosperity returns. All possible crimes, robbery, theft and murder occur almost daily. Although there have been no murders for almost fourteen days, it is still dangerous to walk alone through the streets in the evening. Unexpectedly, one is knocked down with a lead ball attached to a short handle and robbed from behind. A person looted this way was recently found dead in a water-filled ditch. The water was barely a foot deep; he was probably rolled into it while unconscious and drowned miserably. Such a robber is seldom caught, and even then he still has the prospect of evading punishment by all sorts of tricks and schemes. Thus a murderer who recently shot a Negro in the light of day from behind without any reason and in the busiest street of the city, will probably go free despite that he is already sentenced to death on the gallows. This is because in the investigation files a small error on a form has been found. God grant that these terrible conditions, which are probably the aftermath of the war, may soon be over! In some homes and families, however, the turmoil of war and disease has brought very gratifying fruits and in some individuals God's grace has awakened an active inner life. This is particularly the case with many returning soldiers, some of them wounded, who had to go through times of hard and difficult testing. But all of this, although it is so close to me that I have immersed myself completely in our local affairs without intending to do so, cannot interest you to the extent that I should be allowed to fill in the whole letter about it. So I want to break it off, however I would enjoy entering into a detailed account of the present state of affairs in Texas, especially in Galveston. Galveston has become a dear home to me and the longer I am here the less I would choose to exchange it for another. About 10 days ago it has been 11 years since I put my foot on the floor of Texas for the first time. It almost seems unbelievable to me that I have become more than 11 years older since I saw you, my dears, taking leave of you for the last time on that cold winter morning—and yet it is so. How much has changed in these long, yet so short years! How would you find me changed if I now stepped into your midst—I hardly believe that you would recognize your Fritz. And what changes would I find with you! Often I think about it and talk about it, and sometimes it makes my heart ache at such reflections, and sometimes I feel a deep homesickness for you. And yet I feel happy at the same time. I have had times here in Texas where I felt very, very unhappy, where I lost the joy and lust for life, and almost believed to be abandoned by God. Such a time was that which immediately preceded the war. But thank the Lord, I have again found the inner peace that I had almost lost and even though I went through hard battles and bleak days, I can tell you in truth: "I am happy, more, far more than I ever deserved and when I have an earthly wish, it would be to see you again in this life." But I have very little hope, and it will probably have to stay as a wish. As God wants! My profession as a teacher is the life I prefer. What used to be a heavy burden for me is now a pleasure and joy. When I think of my youth, especially the last two years of my living in the old home, it seems almost incomprehensible to me how gracious the dear God has led and directed me. Truly, I do not deserve it, and hardly dare to think of what would have become of me if I had deserved it. Also the noble friends, to whom I owe it after God first, that I was given the opportunity to travel to Texas. I am still more deeply grateful today than I was then. At home my whole career was ruined by my guilt; here I could and did start anew. If

I stayed in Europe I hardly believe that I would still be alive; for, despite some severe and dangerous climatic illnesses, with which I was afflicted in the early years, my physical constitution is far more powerful and enduring than it ever was before. So I can assure you, my dear ones, that aside from the separation from you, which often saddens me enough, especially when I write to you, all the other circumstances in which I stand here contribute to ever new things to warm the heart thanks to God.

This time, which unfortunately could not happen for a long time, I enclose a small bill of exchange addressed to brother Jean. It is 8 pounds sterling, payable by a London auction house. I think the paper will be easy to sell in Basel and should be worth about 200 francs, a little more or less depending on the price of the exchange. I ask dear brother Jean, first of all, to pay the remainder of my old debt from the amount of the exchange, which may not be much. Of the remainder, 50 francs are earmarked for dear sister Henriette, partly as compensation for the expenses, which I have caused her (books and newspapers, etc.), partly so that she can visit my friend Ebinger in Zurich and greet him warmly. I ask you to put 20 francs for my dear niece Louise in her Piggy Bank, although unfortunately I do not even know what the dear child looks like. Please give her a warm kiss in my name. What is left of the money then belongs to the dear, good mother. For any use or convenience of which she certainly needs in her old days. May God bless abundantly the little sign of love that comes from both me and my dear wife, from sincere loving hearts!

For the gifts and souvenirs that actually arrived in the box transported by brother in January, we would like to express our sincere thanks to the dear greatly. The books and newspapers were the most welcome of all, even though the treats and plums were delicious, especially the first ones, which I had not seen for nearly 12 years, and which reminded me of dear old Basel. I have been able to read the newspapers quite well in the past 3 weeks, since I can spend a few hours in the evening for recreation. Then I read through all the advertisements and announcements in the Basler Nachrichten quickly and conscientiously and I am not surprised to find so many unknown and so few known names in them. A whole new generation seems to have grown up, and I can't even find my way around the street names. I have already heard of Wallstrasse; my dear brother's famous palace is supposed to be there—but where is Hammerstrasse, Clarastrasse, etc.? I really believe that if I suddenly arrived in Basel, I could find myself lost in the bright light of day; that happened to me in Galveston only in the darkest of nights.

The flowers from Jean's garden are a dear souvenir on my desk; but I would rather stand in his little garden as a guest, even in heavy rainy weather, just not in your grim cold winter. I can't take it anymore, although here as there in winter it is quite cold. Last winter was the mildest I can remember. On most days I had to keep all ten windows open at school, and heating was necessary only a few times. On the other hand, we often had heavy thunderstorms.

You must excuse me for writing everything mixed up without any order. I write just as my thoughts run, a letter to my mother and brother, to my sister and brother-in-law are a casual conversation, not a well-proportioned essay portioned into appropriate parts and trimmed to size. So it could happen that I suddenly stumble back into writing about my school from writing about Jean's flower garden, which was also supposed to be a vegetable garden too. It occurs to me that I may not have written to you yet, that I've had for more than a year a loyal, dear helper at school. He is a rather old man by the name of Doebner, without whose help I would not have known how to get through the past few months. The total number of pupils amounts to over 150. My old friend Doebner teaches the little ones in the church in German, while in the schoolhouse, I teach the Germans English lessons. This organization has not only made my job easier and more enjoyable, but also fruitful. The school enjoys great respect here and we have to reject new students every day because of lack of space and teaching staff. Unfortunately, I have not yet written to my childhood friend, Pastor Roth. Despite Jean's assurance that he would be pleased to receive a letter from me, I have not got around to it yet. It is very difficult to write for the first time to a friend from whom one has observed constant silence for so many years. In my briefcase there is still a letter that I have begun to him, but the same is dated April 18, 1859. At that time I stopped on the second page, but suddenly felt so discouraged that I was unable to finish it. At that time I did not even know exactly where he was, and whether he had long since forgotten the one-time inseparable friend with whom so many unpleasant memories were connected. Of course, I feel a little different now. Of course I have always preserved his memory with much love and respect; but the fact that he is now working as a deacon at Leonhardskirche, the church where I was baptized and confirmed, makes him dear to me again. Oh, that I could only sit in the study with him for his lesson, how much more could it be said, how much more thoroughly the heart moved, when I sit at my desk for a whole week, the eye is clouded with tears, the pen in hand, but the heart in the home! Dear Jean, be so

View of Galveston circa 1880 from Tremont Hotel, depicting Galveston just four years after Gloor's death. *Courtesy of the Rosenberg Library.*

kind and greet my best dear, dear, sincere friend I have ever held warmly, and tell him how I remember him daily, how I am always grateful to him for all.

His friendship has passed the strong test that it warned of sin and yet he did not despise and disregard those who had fallen to it despite all warnings. Tell him that I will write to him when possible later this month. But, I have to close as the paper is running out. So does the time. I have dated these lines the 18th of April; it has now become the 20th because the day before yesterday I could not write more than a date and heading because I got held up unexpectedly. So I have already missed a post which I wrote to Mr. Epharus Bohnenberger, whom I asked to give you notice that I am sending you a letter with a bill of exchange at the same time. So that I will find out

Photograph of Friedrich Gloor's grave marker at Galveston's Old City Cemetery, engraved with the words, "In memory of the loving friend Friedrich Gloor—born on the 31st of October 1835—died on the 11th of November 1876—pastor of the evangelical Lutheran community—dedicated by his community and friends—'Where I am, my servant shall also be. John 12:26.'" Gloor's wife, Theresa, is buried next to him. *Courtesy of Daryl Walters.*

soon if the letter became lost. Thank God that the postal service is open again, and his letters are no longer sent on such dangerous secret paths through Mexico, Havana etc.!

My dear wife sends you all warm greetings.

Greetings to all who ask for me, especially to the family Stocklin, Maeglin, to the dear Mr. Gysin & family, Mr. Pfr. Legrand, Mr. Spittler & Jaeger, teacher Mr. Schaeublin, who, like me was found in the newspaper, your neighbor Mr. Meister in the Land Orphanage. Be also you, dear mother, brother, sister, also you, unknown wife, sister-in-law and your little ones, warmly greeted and kissed / by your son & brother Friedrich Gloor.

[Along the left margin of the first page: *"Enclosed also a confederate 20 and 10 dollar note, which are now completely worthless, but can serve as a souvenir of the war time."*]

NOTES

1. *Journal of Ecclesiastical History* 73, no. 3 (July 2022), published by Cambridge University Press.
2. Nelson E. Clifford, *The Lutherans in North America* (Philadelphia, PA: Fortress Press, 1980).
3. Benjamin Springler, Ms. L.G. Sanders, A.C. Becker and Donald Bell, Anniversary Booklet committee, *One Hundredth Anniversary First Ev. Lutheran Church, Galveston, Texas (1850–1950)*.
4. Bishop Mike Rinehart, *History of the Lutheran Church, Ministry on the Frontier* (N.p.: Texas-Louisiana Gulf Coast Synod, Evangelical Lutheran Church in America), www.gulfcoastsynod.org; *A History of the Lutheran Church in Texas* (N.p.: South Texas Printing Company, 1954).
5. *A Brief Review of the Past and Survey of the Present of the First Evangelical Lutheran Church of Galveston* [Texas] *Diamond Jubilee Celebration, November 8, 9, 10 and 11, 1925*, page 9, Active ELCA Congregation file—First Lutheran Church, Galveston, Texas, ELCA Region 4-South Archives, Seguin, Texas. Available online at swtSynod.pastperfectonline.com.
6. Ibid.
7. Courtesy of the University Library of Basel, G IV 117.
8. Gloor's original writings in Swiss German, translated to English here, are shown in standard typeface, and manuscript notes providing clarification and summarization are shown in italics.
9. Friedrich's first letter was never discovered.

10. This letter has been edited from the original writing. The complete English translation exists at the Basel University Library website, 16 Briefe an Eltern und Geschwister (swisscollections.ch).

11. This letter has been edited from the original writing. The complete English translation exists at the Basel University Library website, 16 Briefe an Eltern und Geschwister (swisscollections.ch).

ABOUT THE TRANSLATOR/AUTHOR

Fred Harley Huddleston was born in Abington, Pennsylvania, in 1950 and soon moved to Houston. He graduated from Texas A&M University with a degree in architecture. His passion was history, particularly historic restoration architecture. He moved to Galveston in 1998 and became a respected restoration architect, contributing his talents to many of Galveston's historic properties, including First Lutheran's Lyceum Building.

Fred's ancestors became members of First Evangelical Lutheran Church in the 1850s. His grandfather Dr. Otto Fred Schoenvogel married at First Lutheran in 1918 and taught Fred a bit of German, and he studied German in high school as well. The internet was also extremely helpful during his translation work.

Fred's knowledge of Galveston, which he obtained through his work as a historic restoration architect and serving on various commissions to preserve Galveston's rich history, also provided resources to understand and translate Friedrich's letters. After beginning these translations, Fred was able to travel to Basel, Switzerland, with his family and walk the same grounds where Friedrich began his life and studies.

The slow process of these translations enlightened Fred to a deeper understanding of the history of Galveston and created a connection with Friedrich and his life in the mid-nineteenth century.

Fred Harley Huddleston, the translator of these letters, passed away on February 11, 2023, before he was able to finalize his work. I am Clay

Rogers, Fred's husband. We shared the fascinating facts in these letters over the last several years. We would often speculate on the secret that haunted Friedrich Gloor.

Fred had substantially completed the work to which he joyfully devoted so much of his time over the last years. I have completed the finishing touches. Fred was a lover of history, his family and Galveston. I hope these letters and this work will help to keep Fred Huddleston's legacy alive, as well as that of Friedrich Gloor.